The Glory of Blood, Sweat & Tears

Dorothy McRae-McMahon

The Glory of Blood, Sweat & Tears

Liturgies for living and dying

JBCE

The Joint Board of Christian Education
Melbourne

Published by
THE JOINT BOARD OF CHRISTIAN EDUCATION
65 Oxford Street, Collingwood 3066, Australia

THE GLORY OF BLOOD, SWEAT AND TEARS:
LITURGIES FOR LIVING AND DYING

© Dorothy McRae-McMahon 1996

This publication is copyright. Other than for the purposes and subject to the conditions prescribed under the Copyright Act, no part of it may in any form or by any means (electronic, mechanical, microcopying, photocopying, recording or otherwise) be reproduced, stored in a retrieval system or transmitted without prior written permission from the publisher.

Limited permission is granted to a purchaser of this book to reproduce copies of a service for use in a local congregation only.

National Library of Australia
  Cataloguing-in-Publication entry.

McRae-McMahon, Dorothy, 1934-

  The glory of blood, sweat and tears: liturgies for living and dying

  Includes index
  ISBN 1 86407 161 3

  I. Liturgies 1. Joint Board of Christian Education
  II. Title
264

First printed 1996.

Design: Kelvin
Cover photography: Kelvin Young, Northside Productions
Typeset by JBCE in Janson Text
Printing: Gill Miller Press

JB96/3775

CONTENTS

Introduction 7

Beginnings
To honour the birthing 11
Being born again 15
Declaration of purpose for a marriage 18
Beginning a new journey together 20
Take this moment 23
Community born in courage 26
Gathering in spirit and in justice 30
Threads in the weaving
   To begin a year or a task 33

Hours in our Days
The hour of expectation 39
The hour of our grieving 42
The hour of nurture 44
The hour of faith and rest 48
The hour of aloneness 50
The hour of community 52
The hour of the call 55
The hour of risk
   For those who want to share in God's work but find it hard 57
The hour of moving 59

Liturgy for . . .
Liturgy for Australia 65
Liturgy for prayer (And so we pray)
   For those who don't always find it easy to pray 69
Mission: the holy ground of God 72
Liturgy for Easter 1 76
Liturgy for Easter 2
   A journey from Good Friday to Easter Day 80

The Journey in Between

Hold your heads high: our liberation is at hand 87
Carriers of a hope
> *A service for people who work together* .89

The feast of God
> *Agape meal* 92

The golden ones
> *A Eucharist for people who feel marginalised* 96

Honour God with your offering 100
Service for healing
> *For a group of people who feel wounded or betrayed* 103

We are the ones who are loved
> *A celebration of our freedom to play* 106

Wash our feet 109
...And the dance goes on 112

Endings

Grieving the child
> *A service for those whose child has a disability* 117

A simple funeral 121
In the end: there is a passion 125

Index of themes 129

Index of resources for worship 130

This book is dedicated to:

Ali, who makes my life journey significant every day.

My son Christopher, who was brain-damaged by his polio vaccination, a casualty to the genuine struggle for human progress, part of the passion of life.

My son Robert, who refuses to give up his dream as an artist and musician in exchange for economic security.

My daughter Lindy, who never lies and meets life head on.

My daughter Melissa, who refuses to settle for other people's thoughts and goes on exploring the universe of experience, imagination and ideas.

The Sydney staff of the National Assembly of the Uniting Church in Australia, especially Margaret Tasker, who affirm my journey and let me explore liturgical possibilities for affirming the significance of our journey together.

Introduction

If I was asked 'What is the most important ministry we can offer to each other?', I would say that it has to do with honouring each others' life journeys as truly significant - whether it be an individual or corporate journey.

If there is one thing I have recognised in those with whom I have journeyed, it is the human tendency to think that our pains, struggles, labouring and joys and remarkable survivals are insignificant.

There was a moment in my life when I was in personal grief and crisis. It came to a head on a Saturday afternoon and I had the responsibility of bringing the Word to the people on the next morning. I lay on my bed and wept. I said to God 'How can I do it?' The lectionary passage was John 17:20-26. As I was lying there, I was visited by a God who said, 'I am one with you, travelling through this grief. You can choose whether you will be one with me.' The phone rang. It was the young woman who was to be the worship leader in the morning. She said 'Dorothy, I feel as though I am there to especially support you tomorrow. Why would I be feeling like that?' I cried and told her why, then drove to her house for comfort and coffee.

As I returned home, I found myself pondering on the meaning of 'the glory' of Christ. As I drove into my driveway, an inner voice said to me, 'Look at the vine leaves and you will see the glory'. I looked and saw the blood red vine leaves climbing across the front of my house with the sun shining through them. 'The glory lies between the dying and the rising,' said the voice. I saw, as perhaps never before, that the glory of life has to do with the passion of human existence - the passionate grief, struggle, pain, caring, protesting, anger, delight, labouring and dancing of our journey.

The next day, I brought the congregation the two simple words I had been given in those moments, then sat down and quietly wept among them. The service went on respectfully as my own life journey was seen as vulnerable and significant. I gave thanks to God for people who could offer that to me.

The liturgies in this book arise out of significant moments in many human journeys. They are mostly brief and simple. They travel from the honouring of the birthing to a very simple funeral - journeys which belong to individuals and group journeys, all of which join us with the great human continuum of life and death. These are liturgies and rituals for groups of ordinary people who are committed to life together and the rigour of the community of human struggle to transform the world. They are all attempts to be honest about the human experience and to trust that our God, who has travelled that way ahead of us, affirms this honesty; indeed, calls us on to have the courage to be authentic in trusting relationship with each other and with Godself.

In offering these liturgies to others, I am handing them over for their improving, evolving and adapting so that they become authentic for those who use them. I also offer them as examples of the attempt to bring into being liturgies which arise from the life of this place, this culture and this time and as an encouragement for others to do the same.

Dorothy McRae-McMahon

Beginnings

*We celebrate
the miracles of grace which change us,
born from the womb of God
and the deeply respected struggles
of our bodies, minds, hearts and souls,
surrounded by costliness,
yet free for us
in the journey towards abundant life.*

TO HONOUR THE BIRTHING

OPENING SENTENCES

Leader: We honour a passage of life:

People: **A beginning of life,
a nurturing of life
and a bringing to birth.**

Leader: A conceiving
a carrying
and a labouring.

People: **We celebrate this journey.
We give our thanks to God.**

SONG *(optional)*

THE CONCEIVING

Voice 1: To conceive is to hope
that something could be.

Voice 2: To conceive is to dare
to become part of a new possibility.

Voice 3: To conceive is to join with another
giving something of oneself
that newness can be born.

Leader: These our friends *(name of woman, name of partner)*
entered this journey of hope.

All: **Thanks be to God!**

(A symbol of beginning is placed in the centre e.g. the woman and her partner bring their own small candles to a table and light another candle together or each place some seeds in a bowl of earth.)

THE CARRYING

Leader: New life is a gift for the nurturing and carrying.

Voice 1: This woman's body was the womb space,
the compassion* and the faithfulness.

Voice 2: She carried the growing weight,
shared her nourishment with this life
and stretched her skin to hold its body.

Voice 3: She felt the small stillness
in the waiting of the early times
and discovered the small flutterings
moving deeply within herself.

Voice 1: In her was the kicking
and the turning and the playfulness,
some of it delightfulness
and some it far less than that!

Voice 2: Her body changed in this experience
and will never be the same again.
There was the aching and the pressure,
the swelling and the awkwardness.

Voice 3: Her body groaned and was tired.
Her body grew its warm cushioning
for the protecting of the life within.

Leader: She was splendid in her fullness
and committed to the cherishing,
and she needed her companions,
the carers on the way.

(The woman stands in the centre and names those who were her supporters.)

Leader: There was a long waiting,
a long preparing.

(silent reflection, during which music is played)

READINGS AND/OR POEMS

'Compassion' in Hebrew, literally means 'womb space'

THE BIRTHING

(The people gather around the woman with her birth companion/s and make contact with her.)

Leader: The long waiting ended
with its anxious and hopeful approaches.
She searched her body for the new signals
as the child weighed heavy within her.
She rehearsed the unknown journey ahead,
holding hard to those who loved her.

Voice 1: And then the dull new rhythm,
the sharp new rhythm,
the labouring away,
the brief rests and strong energy.

Voice 2: On and on, no ending, no stopping,
the pulsing forces engaging all she had,
more than all she had.
The sounds of pain and energy
flowed from her,
gathering her strength for the struggle for life.

Voice 3: Dreadful and glorious,
she moved with it and worked with it,
deeply connected with the great explosive momentum
of the creation itself and its Creator.

Leader: And then the birthing took its own power,
subsuming her body in pain,
in blood, in the waters.
Who can tell the difference then
between living and dying?
In the relentlessness, the endlessness,
the agony, the ecstasy,
the tearing and the bleeding, the wonder and the joy,
as life emerges
and frees itself at last from its mother-body.

(The people place hands on the woman in silence.)

Leader: Let us stand back and honour the birthing.

(The people move back in a circle.)

THANKSGIVING AND HONOURING

Leader: This is the moment
in the life of this woman
and those who love her *(the partner can be named here)*
which can never be repeated.
It is unique.
Let us mark, honour,
and give thanks for the miracle of this birthing:

All: **We affirm and give thanks
for hope in the conceiving
and faithfulness in the cherishing.
We honour in this woman
the courage,
the energy,
the endurance
and the pain which carried this child into birth.
Here we name a miracle.
Here we claim our being made in the image of God
as those whose bodies
can be the pathways to life.
Thanks be to this woman
and thanks be to God.
Amen.**

SONG

BLESSING

Leader: Go in peace
and ponder in you hearts,
as did Mary of Nazareth,
the wonder of this moment.
And may God the Creator
go on creating in us,
Christ the sustainer
cherish all our fullnesses of life;
and the Spirit break forth in us
in its eternal newness.

All: **Amen.**

This liturgy is for Lindy, Scotty and Brook, the new little stream of life who was born in this birthing.

BEING BORN AGAIN

OPENING SENTENCES

Leader: Just when we think nothing new could be found in us,
all things known, all things gone as far as they can go:

People: **You are born again within us,
God of new beginnings.**

Leader: Just as we think nothing can ever change,
all things established, embedded in old powers:

People: **The transforming flow of your life is there among us,
God of new ways of being.**

Leader: Just when the deathly cycles
drag us down into nothingness,
all things despairing, all things destroying:

People: **You rise in vivid life beyond our weak survivals,
God of new victories over death.
Thanks be to God.**

SONG

WE WERE NOT EXPECTING A MIRACLE

Leader: Most of us were not expecting a miracle, O God.
Some of us were expecting a miracle,
but not for us.

(silent reflection)

Leader: Many things hold us back from new possibilities:

*(The people share the things that hold them back.
Alternatively, the leader speaks the following lines:)*
fear of what it would mean to change,
the power of our past relationships in life,
things which have happened to us,
things which we have done or not done,
and discouragement
because we often cannot see
too many signs of your reign
in us and in the world.

(silent reflection)

Leader: We would like to expect miracles, O God.

People: **Please give us faith,
and help us in our unbelief.**

ASSURANCE

Leader: The Word to us in Christ is that
if we have faith as much as a mustard seed,
that will be enough
for the transforming of us and the world.

People: **Thanks be to God.**

READINGS

Including John 3: 1-16

TESTIMONY

*The person or people share experiences of being born again.
Music or dance of celebration.
Those involved are encircled by the community of faith and
anointed as the royal children of God :*

Leader: Lift your faces to God and those who love you.
You are born again in the power of the Spirit.

People: **Thanks be to God!**

AFFIRMATION OF FAITH

Leader: In response to the Word, let us celebrate our faith :

All: **We celebrate
the miracles of grace which change us,
born from the womb of God
and the deeply respected struggles
of our bodies, minds, hearts and souls,
surrounded by costliness,
yet free for us
in the journey towards abundant life.**

**We celebrate
the moments when we are turned around
and look on ourselves and the world
as though we make new entry
and a different start
with living water for our thirst
and life-giving bread for our hunger.**

We celebrate
the wonder of a creation
in which nothing is limited
to our horizons of sight
or boundaries of energy, courage or hope
but which leaps forth
in amazing surprises of good
and endless transformations
towards its true fullness
in the imagination of God.

INTERCESSION

Leader: Hold this new birth in us, O God.

People: **Keep it safe for growing.**

Leader: Sustain this new faith in us, O God.

People: **Keep it strong for hoping.**

Leader: Direct this new power in us, O God.

People: **Keep it only for good.**

Leader: Cherish this new freedom in us, O God.

People: **Keep it true for the transformation of the world, in your name.
Amen.**

SONG

BLESSING

Leader: Go in joy,
to sing with the whole creation
of the glory of God.
And God the Creator be the source of our life,
God in Christ rise in our midst
and the Spirit be wise in our ways.

All: **Amen.**

DECLARATION OF PURPOSE FOR A MARRIAGE

Marriage is born of the earth.
Two people in partnership,
companions on the road,
feet and soul planted firm in reality,
living free from truth
in mutual fidelity and respect
and expanding in the nurturing of love.

Marriage is a sacred trust
between two people
who dare to live in flight,
carried by winds of creativity
wherever life and growing may take them,
holding hard to each other
with arms stretched out to the world
in openness,
born of loving hospitality,
choosing to embrace others
in the overflowing generosity
from their journey together.

Marriage is a humble, vulnerable travelling,
lived deep in the healing waters of forgiveness,
washed clean by things
left behind in grace,
flowing on to open seas
with waves and tides
of unknown life,
each one sheltering in the safety of the other.

Marriage is the deep-burning life of fire,
two lovers refined in the passion of life together,
each for the other a source of warmth and light
in moments of shadow,
a fire which burns with life, not death,
rising ever free on the holy ground of love.

Like the earth, wind, water and fire,
marriage lives strong
in the endless possibilities for new creation,
held in the hands of God who made it,
walking with the Christ,
who never leaves it nor forsakes it
and dancing free to the song of the Spirit
who delights in its celebration.

Written for Trisha Watts and Peter Solness on the occasion of their marriage.

BEGINNING A NEW JOURNEY TOGETHER

OPENING SENTENCES

Leader: The hand of God encircles us:
People: **God of our beginnings holding us firm.**
Leader: The feet of Christ walk before us:
People: **God of our journeying showing us the way.**
Leader: The wings of the Spirit lift us up:
People: **God who is our company, our energy, our joy.**

SONG

FACING THE UNKNOWN

Leader: We may bring some vulnerable things to a new
fear of the unknown,
a sense of inadequacy,
loneliness in a new group,
anxieties about coping with what lies ahead,
perhaps tiredness or unreadiness.
Let us, in faith and trust,
share those things with each other
and be joined in our humanness:

(The people name the more vulnerable things they bring to the journey.)

Leader: Jesus, remember us, as we take up the grave responsibility of being the church.

All: *(sung three times)*
'Jesus, remember us, when you come into your kingdom'
(Taizé)

THE ASSURANCE

Leader: Hear the word in Christ to us:
Nothing in all creation can separate us
from the love of God.
Rise up and walk in faith.

All: **Amen.**

THE WORD

AFFIRMATION OF FAITH

Leader: Let us respond to the word by affirming our faith:

All: **We believe in God
who created us from nothing
and goes on bringing to birth
new things beyond our imagining.**

**We believe in Jesus Christ
who entered our unknown journey
and experienced all our living,
who walked in our earthiness
and can still be discovered
in our midst.**

**We believe in the Holy Spirit
who calls us on to truth
in light beyond our seeing,
who stirs within our being
like a melody of possible music,
who dances on before us
in the freedom of passionate life.**

SHARING OUR HOPES BEFORE GOD

Leader: As we begin this journey together,
let us share our hopes and light a small candle
as a sign that the light of Christ travels with us
in these hopes:

(Each person names a hope or expectation for their journey and lights a candle.)

Leader: Now let us remember the hopes of the world and the communities we have left behind:

(The people share their prayers for others.)

Leader: O God, we place this our life in your hands.

People: **Take all that we bring,
our gifts and talents,
our longings and our faith
and add your power for life
for we ask it in the name of Jesus Christ.
Amen.**

THE COMMITMENT TO EACH OTHER

Leader: As we are able, let us make our commitment to walk together on this journey:

All: **We will walk this way together,
with Jesus Christ in our midst.
Our hands are open to receive,
our hearts are open to give,
our minds long to learn
and our souls reach out to each other.
This time is eternal time for us
and God will be our blessing.
Amen.**

SONG

DISMISSAL

Leader: Go into this moment in faith
and may the Holy God prepare a holy ground for you,
Christ Jesus take your hand on the way
and the Spirit surround you
with a cloud of grace.

All: **Amen.**

TAKE THIS MOMENT

GREETING
Leader: The peace of Christ be with you.

People: **And also with you.**

TAKE THIS MOMENT
Leader: God who lives beyond our time
before our beginnings and after our endings:

People: **Take this our moment.
It belongs to you.**

Leader: God who entered our time in Jesus
and made new things possible:

People: **Take this our moment.
It belongs to you.**

Leader: God who goes ahead of time,
like wind and flame before us :

People: **Take this our moment.
It belongs to you.**

SONG
(Suggest 'Take this Moment' by John Bell, Iona Community)

THE LAYING DOWN
Leader: Dear God,
sometimes our painful moments
become the whole of life for us,
overwhelming our memories of good times,
distorting our view of life
and your faithfulness to us.

People: **We place our moments in your healing hands.**

Leader: Sometimes our moments become so much our own that
we forget that they belong also to others and to you.

People: **We place our moments in your hands for sharing**.

Leader: Sometimes we race through life
losing precious moments
which we are given as gifts.

People: **Take these moments and return them to us.**

Leader: O God, if there are other things
which we do not need to carry with us
because they would be burdens for the next journey.

People: **We lay them down in faith.**
Amen.

THE ASSURANCE

Leader: Hear the word of assurance:
The Body of Christ
has already received all that we lay down in faith.
We are free again to live and move on in resurrected life.

People: **Amen.**

THE WORD

Ephesians 1: 15-19

THE AFFIRMATION

Leader: Let us affirm our faith.

All: **We believe**
that every moment of our life
is important to God.
Every struggle is honoured,
every pain is felt,
every courage is celebrated
and every small victory
is marked with delight.

We believe
that every moment of our life
is held precious,
walked in by Jesus Christ
as though our experience
is worth knowing,
and our choices
are worth making.

We believe
that every moment of our life
could possibly hold
the dancing Spirit of God,
as though we are part

of a great adventure,
**the loved ones of the passion
whose every moment
could be a moment of grace.**

PRAYERS FOR THE NEXT MOMENT

Leader: In this moment of leaving one part of the journey behind,
we need your light and life for the next moments.
Keep us in your care, O God, as we walk forward again.
We ask for these gifts for our journey.

(The people name the gifts that are needed.)
Hold us fast, God of love.

People: **Keep your vision before us, God of hope,
and be at our centre, God of peace.**

All: **Amen.**

THE SENDING

Leader: This is the moment of leaving this place
and being sent forth again into the world.
Are we ready to go?

People: **In faith, we are ready.
We will go forth into the known and unknown,
open to new things
and trusting in the company of God.**

(If some people are taking up a particular task, they can be given special gifts for the journey from the rest of the community of faith.)

BLESSING

Leader: Go in faith:
the journey is in God's hands.
And may the winds of the Spirit blow free,
the courage of the Christ be deep within you
and the great Creator bring new life before you.

All: **Amen.**

For my friend John Bell of the Iona Community, who takes so many moments and turns them into liturgy and song for the world.

COMMUNITY BORN IN COURAGE

THE GREETING

Leader: The peace of Christ be with you.

People: **And also with you.**

OPENING SENTENCES

Leader: Your love is filled with courage, O God.

People: **You pursue your people down the ages, calling us forth with the rigour of prophetic word.**

Leader: Your love is filled with courage, O Christ.

People: **Courage which stands in our death and announces the power of costly life.**

Leader: Your love is filled with courage, Holy Spirit.

People: **It leaps beyond our fear and burns with the flame of your passion for truth. Thanks be to God!**

SONG

WE ARE AFRAID

Leader: It is easy to speak of loving each other, O God,
and easy to imagine that we mostly do.
Yet the uneasy spaces of words not said,
feelings not shared, convictions not stated,
or thoughts which run among us ill-directed,
become like deep valleys of separation
hidden in polite smiles
and the rush of our busyness.

(silent reflection)

We do not want to hurt each other,
we fear the loss of love,
we run very short of energy to cope with truth
and often we wonder whether it matters after all.

People: **Call us gently, O God.**
Cast out our fear, O God.
Give us the gift of trust
and the safety of our love for each other
and your love for us all.

THE ASSURANCE

Leader: Hear the word for us today:
Do not fear, for I have redeemed you;
I have called you by name, you are mine.
When you pass through the waters,
I will be with you;
and through the rivers, they shall not overwhelm you;
when you walk through the fire you shall not be burned,
and the flame shall not consume you. (Isaiah 43:1a-2)

All: **Amen.**

THE WORD

Psalm 121

(silent reflection)

AFFIRMATION OF FAITH

Leader: In response to the word, let us affirm our faith:

All: **In the emptiness of eternity,**
even our emptiness,
God's creative power blossomed
in infinite patterns of uniqueness
and infinite flowerings of good.

In ordinary things,
including us,
God's Word for the world
emerges in faithfulness,
stark in its frailty
and beautiful in surprising strength.

In vulnerable lives,
such as our own,
God's Spirit lives and moves,
calling us beyond the commonplace,
bravely struggling to be,

**reborn in every costly moment
when we are true and free and full of love.**

GOD IS WITH US

Leader: We are very glad you are with us, O God.
There are times when it feels
as though there might be no-one else.
Sometimes it seems as though you too have left us alone.
But here, together, we claim your company in faith
and ask you to travel with us through this day and our lives.
These are the special gifts we need,
O God who gives in grace,

(The people name the gift they need most and give a flower to another person.)

We bless you for all your loving care for us, O God.

All: *(sung)* **'Bless the Lord, my soul, and bless God's holy name.'** *(Taizé)*

SONG

BLESSING

Leader: Go into this day in peace.
And may the breath of God bring life to all we do,
the grace of Christ stand clear within our humanness
and the Spirit lighten our hearts with delight.

All: **Amen.**

This service can be used as the basis of a retreat for people who work together and need courage to be honest with each other. They can be asked to spend a time in silence after the service and reflect on the following questions, then return and share together with courage.

QUESTIONS FOR REFLECTION

1) **In what areas of my life and work do I most need the gift of courage?** *(Be very specific in this reflection.)*
   Imagine the situations.
   Picture the people involved.

2) **What lies at the centre of your fear?**
   What could happen to you?
   What might you lose?

3) **What would give you courage?**
   What support do you need?
   Whose support do you need?

4) **Is there some brave step you could take now?**
   What good could flow from this step?
   What peace with yourself could follow?

GATHERING IN SPIRIT AND IN JUSTICE

GREETING
Leader: Christ be with you.

People: **And also with you.**

THE GATHERING
Leader: Christ is our light.

People: **And we gather with that light in our midst.**

Leader: We sing in the symbols of our time and place
and place them on the table as a sign
that we have not moved away from them
in our life together.

People: *(The people sing something like* 'The Lord is our light, our light and salvation . . .' *from Taizé as the symbols are brought in, singing softly as each symbol is announced.)*

Reader 1: Here is the sign of the original people
who loved this land.
(Aboriginal symbols are placed on the table.)

People: **The Lord is our light . . .**

Reader 2: Here are signs of some of those who came later.
(Symbols of different ethnic groups are placed on the table.)

People: **The Lord is our light . . .**

Reader 3: This is a sign of the beauty of the creation
in which we live.
(A branch of a native tree is placed on the table.)

People: **The Lord is our light . . .**

Leader: We are all here, together with welcome guests
who are visiting us.
Let us say our names together and claim our place
in this our gathering in Spirit and in justice.
(The people say their own names together.)

People: **The Lord is our light . . .**
(The candle is carried in, in silence, and lit.)

Leader: Let us celebrate this moment!

People: *(sung) The people sing the* Doxology.

Leader: We are the people who are called to the feast.
Thanks be to God for the gifts of each other,
the food and those whose hands prepared it.

A MEAL IS SHARED

The people are regathered as some begin to sing:

SONGS OF HOPE

THE WORD
Readings

FOCUSED PRESENTATION ON A SOCIAL JUSTICE THEME

The people reflect in silence on their response to the word and then share in small groups, concentrating on ideas for action.

The people are regathered as someone begins to sing.

INTERCESSION

Leader: What are our longings for the church and the world?

(The people say words and phrases to express their longings.)
At intervals the leader will say:
O Christ, hear our prayer.

Response: *(sung)* 'O Lord, hear our prayer, O Lord hear our prayer…' *(Taizé)*

OFFERING

SHARINGS FOR THE FUTURE

The groups share their ideas for action.

SONG

COMMISSIONING AND SENDING OUT

Leader: We are called to share with God
in the response to our longings.

People: **We are the children of God.**
We have heard the groaning of the whole creation.
In faith we will emerge
as the ones who act in hope.

Leader: We are not alone.

People: **We will return to the communities**
from which we have come
carrying the light of Christ with us.

(The candle is carried out.)

We will travel with God
and those who gather anywhere
in Spirit and in justice.
Amen.

BLESSING

Leader: Go now and take your place on holy ground.

People: **All God's creation is holy ground.**

Leader: May peace be your dream,
justice be your vision on the way,
and God's freedom open before you
like a pathway of hope.

All: **Amen.**

THREADS IN THE WEAVING
To begin a year or a task

GREETING

Leader: Peace be with you.

People: **And also with you.**

OPENING SENTENCES

Leader: Here we begin another year,
weaving together the fabric of our life,

People: **in all its different colours and textures,
in all its changing form and flow.**

Leader: Here we mark the things which have gone before,

People: **and hope for the newness to come.**

Leader: Here we celebrate each one as a thread in the weaving,

People: **here we cherish the moments
when the fabric of our life becomes whole.**

SONG

LET US NOT PRETEND

Leader: Let us not pretend that, as we see our life as a weaving,
there are no tears, mends, holes and knotted places:
silent hurts and angers which make sad gaps
in our relationships;

(silent reflection)

threads of lives moving in opposition to each other,
or pulled so tightly they nearly break,
thin patches and frayed edges of tiredness,
disappointments or failed expectations that fade the fabric
and discolour its beauty.

(silent reflection)

We are very human, O God.

People: **Give to us your grace,
give to us your loving forgiveness.
Amen.**

ASSURANCE

Leader: God is present in grace among us,
woven within our lives,
like a strong golden thread
of transforming possibilities.
We are forgiven!

People: **Thanks be to God.**

(A golden thread is placed on a cloth on the floor in the centre.)

READINGS

THE CELEBRATION

Leader: We celebrate each thread
that makes up the pattern of our life together.
Let us think of words which describe ourselves;
choose a thread and place it on the floor
as part of the weaving:

(The people share in making the 'weaving'.)

Let us think of those other threads
which contribute to our life
because they are our visitors, our friends
and those who support and serve us:

(People name others and select threads for them.)

AFFIRMATION AND COMMITMENT

Leader: Here is beauty, here is variety,
many things can be created from this fabric:

All: **We are a cloth of diverse colours,
made from many gifts and graces.
We are the people flowing forth from the Creator,
surprising ourselves
with the things which can be done.**

**We are raw material
for rewarding relationships
as our lives interweave,
contributing one to the other,
holding each other firm
when one is weak or breaking.**

**We are each worthy of being respected and cared for,
essential to the pattern,**

skilled in our appointed tasks,
vehicles for unexpected wisdom and skills,
sources of laughter and sharers of tears,
working with each other that, one day,
this world may be a place
where all people live in justice, freedom and peace.

This is our hope, this is our faith,
Christ Jesus will be our company
and the Spirit gives life to the weaving.

INTERCESSION

Leader   We dedicate our work to you.

People: **Go with us into this year, O God.
Take all that we offer and add to that your gifts.
Breathe into our work your energy,
truth and courage,
that we may be faithful, humble people
who are truly gracious to each other
and truly committed to the vision of life
with which you call us on.
Amen.**

SONG

THE COMMISSIONING

The worship leader takes a scarf (or length of fabric) and places it around the shoulders of the first person, with the words:

Leader: Remember your calling.

That person passes it on to the next person with the same words.

BLESSING

Leader: Go into this year in peace.

People: **We go in faith.**

Leader: And may the loving-kindness of God be found among us,
the humanness of Christ make gentle our paths
and the Spirit sing songs of hope in our hearts.

All: **Amen.**

Hours in our Days

PHOTO RHONDA MILNER

*We believe in God
who takes our smallest moment of hope
and grows it forth like a tree
with spreading branches
for the sheltering of new life.*

THE HOUR OF EXPECTATION

OPENING SENTENCES

Leader: Like a moment of truth it comes mid-life:

People: **And we can pause for it, or presume to know.**

Leader: Like a stirring of unease,
it comes as a warning of new things:

People: **And we can feel a possibility or go firmly past.**

Leader: The moment belongs to us now
and we can cup the hands of our soul in open invitation:

People: **Waiting expectantly for the gifts of the Spirit of God.**

(silent reflection)

SONG

IT IS HARD TO KEEP EXPECTING

Leader: It is hard to keep expecting the coming of the Christ.
We look at each other, we look at our world
and we wonder whether it is all an illusion.
Let us share the things which we see:

(The people name those things in their places of work which seem to blot out the hope of the reign of God.)

Leader: Our faith runs low and sometimes we feel
there can be nothing new enough, O God.

People: *Sung response, or*
**Nothing new enough,
nothing powerful enough,
nothing loving enough, O God.**

ASSURANCE

Leader: Hear the Word in Jesus Christ:
Whether we can see it, or not,
the victory is already won!
Life has conquered death.
The old order has passed away
and the new order has begun.
Receive the gift of hope.

People: **Thanks be to God!**

READINGS

SONG

THE WORD IS AMONG US.

We share with each other a hope for their work or their meeting.

SONG

AFFIRMATION OF FAITH

All: **We believe in God
who takes our smallest moment of hope
and grows it forth like a tree
with spreading branches
for the sheltering of new life.**

**We believe in Jesus Christ
who walks tall among us,
seen in our faces, felt in our hearts,
bedded deep in the longing of our souls
for all that is true, just and full of love.**

**We believe in the Holy Spirit
who waits on our moments of openness
and springs into the unknowns
with joy and delight,
that we might be called on
beyond where we thought we could go,
where every step is walked on holy ground.**

INTERCESSION

Leader: The city, the holy ground of God:
Let us pray for each sign of holiness
which we have seen.

(The people share the signs they have seen and light a small candle or place a flower in a bowl.)

At intervals the Leader will say:

Leader: We place these signs of hope in your hands, O God.

People: **Keep them safe for the people of your city.**

Leader: There are always more signs of your presence
than we had remembered, O God of grace.

> Take our lives together here
> and lift up your risen life among us,
> that we may be your faithful people
> and you may be our God.

People: **Amen.**

SONG

BLESSING

Leader: Go in peace and faith.
> If you are tired, may you find rest.
> If you are anxious, may you find peace.
> If you are lonely, may you find friends
> and if you are dying, may you find new life
> and know that nothing can separate you
> from the love of God in Christ Jesus.

People: **Amen.**

THE HOUR OF OUR GRIEVING

OPENING SENTENCES

Leader: Jesus looked on the city of Jerusalem and wept.

People: **Our tears were your tears, O Christ.**

Leader: And Jesus looked upon Peter and said,
'Before the cock crows, you will betray me three times.'
Peter hid his face and wept.

People: **We weep with Peter for our own betrayals.**

Leader: And the whole creation groaned in labour,
waiting for the sons and daughters of God to emerge.

People: **Pray for us, Holy Spirit,
when we do not even know what to pray.
We grieve for the pain of the world.**

(A bowl of 'tears' is placed in the centre.)
The people remember the tears of the world in silence.

All: *Sung response such as:*
'O Lord hear our prayer, O Lord hear our prayer.' *(Taizé)*

THE WORD

SONG

AFFIRMATION OF FAITH

Leader: In response to the word, let us affirm our faith:

All: **We believe in God,
from whose heart flows forth
healing enough for the pain of the world
and our pain.**

**We believe in Jesus Christ,
who saw into the souls, minds and bodies
of people like us
and reached out in healing touch,
gathering in the wounded ones
in love beyond the commonplace.**

**We believe in the holy Spirit
who breathes warmth
into the cold places,
touches with living fire
the deathliness in our life
and remembers with grief,
all the hurts
which we dare not name.**

REMEMBERING OUR HEALING

Leader: Let us remember moments of healing in the life of the world.

(The people share their memories and place a flower in the bowl of tears.)

Leader: We remember your healing hand, O God.

People: **Come to us again, for we need you now.
Amen.**

SONG

BLESSING

Leader: Go in faith, for there will be a new heaven and a new earth.

People: **There will be no more weeping,
for those who mourn will be comforted
and the poor will inherit the earth.
Come, Lord Jesus. Lord Jesus, come.
Amen.**

THE HOUR OF NURTURE

GREETING
Leader: Christ be with you.

People: **And also with you.**

CALL TO WORSHIP
Leader: Now is the time of the feast!

People: **Call in all the people —
the oppressed, the hungry, the tired —
all who need our company
and the solidarity of God.**

Leader: Our God is generous.
The cup is full to overflowing,
the bread can be shared with all
and the dance of life comes after.

All: **Thanks be to God!
Let us worship in spirit and in truth.**

SONG

CONFESSION
Leader: Your presence, O God,
invites us to know more truly who we are.

(A period of silence while we are open to that knowing)

Leader: The world still waits in hunger and thirst, O God.

People: **Forgive our weakness.
Forgive our lack of faith.**

ASSURANCE OF PARDON
Leader: We worship a God of grace.
The word to us in Jesus Christ is —
Our sin is forgiven!

People: **We celebrate our freedom!
We honour the holiness of God.**

All: 'Hosanna' *or* 'Allelujah' *(sung)*

READINGS
    Old Testament
    New Testament

SONG

THE GOSPEL

THE WITNESSES

(Testimonies of the people)

AFFIRMATION OF FAITH

Leader: In response to the word, let us stand and affirm our faith.

All: **We believe that horizons of hope
are never fixed.
They always move beyond,
in the creativity of God.**

    **We believe that powers of evil
cannot kill God.
God walks on free and leaps off our crosses
in the risen Jesus Christ.**

    **We believe that the Spirit can never be confined.
She dances forth in the world
and is found in surprising places,
leading us on until the end of time.**

PRAYERS OF INTERCESSION

Leader: Let us pray:
Come claim your ground, O holy God
and show us more clearly your standing places.

People: **We long to be one with you there.**

Leader: Where are you among the homeless?
Where are you among the lost?

People: **We long to be one with you there.**

Leader: Where are you among the races?
Where are you among the cultures?

People: **We long to be one with you there.**

Leader: Where are you among the churches?
Where are you among the workers?

People: **We long to be one with you there.**

Leader: On the holy ground of the city
Come claim your people, O God.

People: **We offer ourselves as those who
try to walk with you.
Come create holy ground under our feet.
Amen.**

SONG

THE OFFERTORY

The bread, wine and gifts are brought to the table.

Leader: The work of human hands is respected of God:
the bread, risen in the warm the,
the wine, crushed in its bitter sweetness.
All that we offer is received and transformed
into new possibilities.

People: **Blessed be God forever!**

THE GREAT THANKSGIVING

Leader: The Lord be with you.

People: **And also with you.**

Leader: Lift up your hearts.

People: **We lift them to our God.**

Leader: Let us give thanks to the Lord our God.

People: **It is right to give our thanks and praise.**

Leader: We give thanks to you, God,
for your love for the world.
You look upon us all and name us good.

People: **You conceive in us a thousand possibilities
and carry us on into the timeless struggle
in bringing to birth the reigning of love.**

Leader: We thank you for Jesus Christ
who gave hope to ordinary people like us
and crashed through the boundaries
which separated us from life.

People: **With those who have gone before us
and those who will come after us,
we join the whole creation in the eternal hymn:**
'Holy Holy Holy' *(sung twice)*

THE EUCHARIST CONTINUES …
FINAL THANKSGIVING

All: **We thank you, God,
that you never leave us hungry and thirsty.
We commit ourselves to so living in love
that all are fed and know your gracious community.
Amen.**

SONG

BLESSING

Leader: Go in peace in the power of Christ.
And may food be found beside the road,
living water rise forth in springs around you
and the Spirit restore you in the hard places.

All: **Amen.**

THE HOUR OF FAITH AND REST

OPENING SENTENCES

Leader: This is the hour of faith and rest.
Faith comes as gift. Rest comes as grace.
Let us be open to the moment …

(silence)

The city is gently covered with the night,
the warm arms of God offer it peace.

SONG

(sung softly)

LAYING DOWN THE DAY

Leader: Let us be aware of the things we are carrying
which need to be laid down
for healing and transformation.

(silent reflection)

Let us image all these things as the body of our death
which now becomes absorbed
into the body of Christ's death.
This body is to be cherished and respected.
How will God cherish this vulnerable body?

*(The people say ways in which they would like
to be cherished by God and each other.)*

All: *(sung)* 'Kyrie Eleison' ('Lord, have mercy')

THE WORD

SONG

THE AFFIRMATION

All: **We wait with confidence and claim with faith,
the power of God for the changes that lead to life.
We stand in our present with honest hearts,
for we need no defences
before a gracious God
and a human Christ.**

> We rest with our future
> as those who do not need to know the way.
> It is already trod, already borne,
> already accompanied.
> Its newness will unfold as we move
> into each small standing-place of faith.

INTERCESSION

Leader: Let us ask God to place around the world the things it needs to survive the night.

The people ask and after several petitions the liturgist says:

Leader: Hear our prayer, O living God.

Response: *(Chosen sung response, or:)*
Come to the world in love, O God of grace.

LITANY FOR THE NIGHT

Leader: In the gentle darkness:

People: **you move within our life, O God.**

Leader: Touching the painful places:

People: **with the healing of your restfulness.**

Leader: Carrying the world:

People: **in the womb-space of your love.
Amen.**

SONG

BLESSING

Leader: Go in peace,
and may God hold you safe in sleeping,
Christ Jesus be clear in your waking
and the Spirit bring energy for a new day.

All: **Amen.**

THE HOUR OF ALONENESS

OPENING SENTENCES

Leader: How can it be, O God,
that with the crowds of the city around us,
we are still alone?
How can it be, O God,
that even with those we know around us,
we are still alone?

People: **Are you calling us out from the people?**
Or have we walked away from your presence?

Leader: Are we moving from the old to the new?
Or are we held here by many bondages?

People **Take this lonely place, O God.**
Reveal it now to us as holy ground.

SONG

SYMBOLS OF ALONENESS

The people image their aloneness. (silent reflection)

CHANT

For example, (sung 3 times) 'By night we travel in darkness'
(Taizé)

ASSURANCE

Leader: Nothing can separate us from the love of God
in Christ Jesus.
The darkness is as light to God. Do not be afraid.
We are never alone.

All: **Amen.**

READINGS

SONG

THE WITNESS

Stories of moments of aloneness and discoveries of the company of God and each other.

AFFIRMATION

All: **We believe we move safely
in the spaces of aloneness.
God who created out of nothing
is the word in the emptiness.**

**We believe in the sure travelling
across the pathways of life.
They will become for us the holy way
towards a new community.**

**We believe in the faithfulness of a God
who lived in deserts and wilderness,
who cried out in aloneness
and knew our life in all its truth.**

INTERCESSION

Leader: Let us turn to our neighbours - three people together - and pray for each other.

(The people pray.)

Leader: Let us stand in a circle and be aware of the promise of the power of the Body of Christ which could embrace us in its love and hope, even as we travel in the dark nights of the soul and the confusions of the human journey.

People: **We will be companions on the way.
We will try to be there for each other,
respectful of the spaces for growing,
reaching across the spaces of loneliness.
This is our commitment.
Amen.**

SONG

BLESSING

Leader: Go in the security of the God who gathers us in, as the mother hen gathers her chickens safely under her warm wings.
Go as the loved children of God.

All: **Amen.**

THE HOUR OF COMMUNITY

OPENING SENTENCES

Leader: Let us gather our community around us -
The God of many names:

(The people give their names for God.)
Those who have gone before us:

(The people name their own 'saints' and mentors.)
Those who are with us in the places where we work:

(The people name their colleagues.)
We are surrounded by a cloud of witnesses.
Their love enfolds us with light and fragrance.

(The coals and incense are lit.)
We are living stones in the building
of the holy city of God.

(The basket of stones is placed in the centre.)

SONG

COMMUNITY IS COSTLY

Leader: Community asks of us:
Vulnerability
Laying down of power
Trust
Commitment to others
Accountability
Faithfulness
Giving and receiving of forgiveness
Openness
Acceptance of diversity
Kindness
Risking of ourselves.

(silent reflection)

Leader: O God, we are many times afraid
of our calling to community.

Voice 1: We would prefer to travel without responsibility.

Voice 2: We would rather not risk being hurt.

Voice 3:   We find it more comfortable
to have structures of power.

Voice 4:   We sometimes choose to stay with our guilt
and separate ourselves from your community.

People: **Forgive us, O God, and help us to remember that we are your Body.**

ASSURANCE

Leader: We are always the broken body
but the word to us
is that in Jesus Christ we are made whole
and enough to do the task.

READINGS

CELEBRATION OF COMMUNITY

Leader: We are living stones in the holy city of God.
Let us take a stone and say what sort of stone we are
as we place it in the centre.

(The people name themselves and place a stone on the communion table or in the centre of the group.)

LITANY OF AFFIRMATION

Leader: We are the people of dignity.

People: **We are those who join
the whole communion of saints,
honoured of God
respected by Christ
and befriended by the Holy Spirit.**

Leader: We are the people who weep
for the suffering of the world.

People: **We truly care
about the world in which we live,
even as we feel our lack of power,
and our need for wisdom.**

Leader: We are the people of hope and faith.

People: **Together we will celebrate
the moments of new life.
Together we will work and play.**

**Together we will give thanks
for the gifts along the way.
Amen.**

SONG

BLESSING

Leader: Go in peace.

People: **We go as one people.
We go as the loved children of God.**

Leader: And may God be at our beginning,
Christ be in our centre,
and the Spirit be there in our endings.

People **Amen.**

THE HOUR OF THE CALL

THE CALL

Leader: Where will we hear your voice, O God?

Voice 1: In the least of these my vulnerable ones …

Leader: But they often push us away.
They don't like us very much,
and they are hard to help.

Voice 2: In the least of these my vulnerable ones …

Leader: But the church never gives us enough resources.
We get very tired and can't see the way forward.

Voice 1: I am Aboriginal …
I speak many languages, but often not yours …
I am unemployed …
I am poor …
I am abused and homeless …
In the least of these, my vulnerable ones …

All: **Call us on, Jesus Christ,**
even when we would rather not hear all these voices.
Call us on, for you are the way, the truth and the life.

SONG

THE WORD

THE WITNESS

SONG

THE AFFIRMATION OF FAITH

Leader: In response to the Word, let us affirm our faith:

All: **We believe the call of God**
is an invitation to life.
We can bear to hear it
because it comes to us in grace and loving kindness.
It is safe to hear it
because Jesus Christ stands with us as we listen,
and takes our hand

as we move towards the suffering ones,
the vulnerable ones,
the ones whose voices we hear
in God's call.
We believe that the Spirit of God
will give us the gifts we need,
even though we falter on the way
and only now and then
lift up the cross of Christ.

THE SOUNDS OF THE VOICES

Leader: Whom do we hear most clearly?

(The people name those who call to them.)

Leader: And God said:
Whom will I send?
Who will go for me?

People: **We have heard your call, O God. Send us.**
We will go, dependent upon your help.
Breathe your divine life into our humanness.
Hold us in the hollow of your hand
and place our feet on holy ground.
Walk with us into your future.
Amen.

SONG

BLESSING

Leader: Go as the truly blessed,
covered by the warm wings of the Spirit,
carried in the womb-space of God,
and one with Jesus Christ in all the way.

People: **We will go in faith.**
Amen.

THE HOUR OF RISK
For those who want to share in God's work but find it hard

OPENING SENTENCES

Leader: Sisters and brothers, will we take the risk
of seeing our world through the eyes of God?

People: **With God's help, we will.**

Leader: Will we hear and taste and smell the poor of the earth
and walk towards the Christ who is already there?

People: **With God's help, we will.**

Leader: Will we so believe in the grace of God that
we can dare to feel the longings of the people
mingled with our own frailty?

People: **With God's help, we will.
We are not alone.**

SONG

KNOWING WHO WE ARE

Leader: Let us look upon the world, the holy ground of God,
even as we remember who we are.

(silence)

Leader: We are not heroic, O God.
We are your ordinary people.
Have mercy on us, O God.

All: *(sung twice or said)*
**Have mercy on us, God of grace.
Have mercy on us, God of love.
Have mercy on us, God of understanding.**

ASSURANCE

Leader: Rise, take up your bed and walk.
The Christ is never defeated by our humanness.
Amen.

People: **Thanks be to God!**

READINGS
(silent reflection)

GATHERING OF THOSE WE SEE
Leader: Let us gather in the people and the situations which we see reflected with concern in the eyes of God.

(The people and situations are gathered in.)

NAMING OUR NEEDS
Leader: What do we need from God to hold us into the rigour and passion and cost of this adventure? What would help us take the risk of standing in solidarity with God's children?
(The people name their needs.)

Leader: Come, O Holy Spirit.

All: **Come, O Holy Spirit.**

THE OFFERING
Leader: What have we to offer to God and the world which God loves?

(The people make their offering - sharing their hopes about what they could do in each small way, and making their money gifts.)

Leader: Receive these our gifts, O God.

People: **Take them as you took the loaves and fishes and transform them into overflowing life. Amen.**

SONG

BLESSING
Leader: God is a God who takes infinite risks with people like us. Go in faith and hope to be part of the recreating of the world.

All: **Amen.**

THE HOUR OF MOVING

GREETING

Leader: Christ be with you.

People: **And also with you.**

CALL TO WORSHIP

Leader: God is a pilgrim God.

People: **Though we find secure places, and warmth
in the sunlight of each other,
our God moves on.**

Leader: Christ walks forward to each Jerusalem.

People: **Though we choose the neat solutions
and the pious resolutions,
the Christ walks on.**

Leader: The Spirit flies into the future.
Though we make our plans and publish our reports,
though people praise us and ask us to stay,
the Spirit flies forth into a new day.

All: **Let us worship God.**

SONG

THIS IS WHO WE ARE

Leader: To stay in the place we know is a great temptation,
O God.

People: **Even if it is a failing place,
even if it is a dying place,
especially if it is a comfortable place,
we long to stay.**

(silent reflection)

Leader: Do you understand us and our fears, O God?
Did you ever want to stop moving?

People: **Be with us please, God.
Take us by the hand
for the next step.**

ASSURANCE

Leader: Hear the word to us in Christ:
I am come that you might have life
and have it to the full.
I have taken you by the hand.
Rise up, move
and live with me.
Amen.

People: **Amen.**

READINGS

FIRST STEPS IN OUR MOVING - CELEBRATION OF FAITH

Leader: In response to the Word, let us stand
and celebrate our faith:

All: **We celebrate the one who said:
'Take this cup from me.'
We give thanks for the one who cried out:
'My God, my God, why have you forsaken me?'
We believe that is this One
who walks with us in every step of the way,
who fears what we fear,
who grieves what we grieve,
who wonders how the moving can happen.
In the power of this God,
we know the next small step is possible.
In the loving of this God,
we walk as those who are never alone.
In the faithfulness of this God,
we will find our own faithful moments.
Amen.**

INTERCESSION

(The people gather in a circle and each person is given a length of ribbon.)

Leader: Let us pray for the world we love,
for the world God loves.
Who will we move towards,
in company with God?

(The people name those they would like to move towards and tie their ribbon to a cross in the centre.)

Leader: Let us place ribbons of colour
around the world
and ourselves,
the colour of the great drama of life,
the colour of the mystery of the presence of God,
the colour of celebration.
We and the world are beautiful in the sight of God.

People: **We commit ourselves
to keep moving towards its life
and our own fullness of life.
We look with respect on all our struggles
and the struggles of the world.
We place it all firmly in the hands of God.
Amen.**

SONG

SENDING OUT

Leader: Turn to the person on your right and send that person into the world with a blessing.

(The people bless each other.)

All: *Sing a blessing song or
say the* Grace *together.*

Liturgy for...

*Here we live.
Here we have our being
with those who have gone before
and those who will come after.
Thanks be to God
for the wonder of this place.*

LITURGY FOR AUSTRALIA

OPENING SENTENCES

Leader: And there it is,
  stretching as far as eye can see in its dry glory,
  unconquered land, speaking of eternal things
  in a secret language of its own.
  There it is in its endless rhythms
  and grey-green dressings,
  living in harmonies
  with redness and blue hazes.
  Old, old earth,
  worn down in wind and fire
  and ancient oceans
  spreading to horizons,
  at one with skies and distances
  resisting controls
  and all the plannings of humankind.
  We call it ours,
  but it is its own and God's.
  It chooses its gifts and gives in its own time,
  the eternal time of all the ages of creation.

People: **Here we live.**
  Here we have our being
  with those who have gone before
  and those who will come after.
  Thanks be to God
  for the wonder of this place.

SONG

OUR LONGINGS

Leader: In faith, we add our prayers
  to those which rise like the smoke of many old fires,
  the longings of the people,
  from the beginning of time.
  Let us share our longings for our country:

  (The people share their longings.)

Leader: Our hearts are searching for who we might be, O God.

People: **We long for the signs
of your presence among us,
even us,
who resist the old forms of religion,
who find it hard to say your name,
who wonder if you are really here
among the struggle and harshness,
the ambiguities and the failures.**

Leader: Be present in the centre of our longing, Jesus Christ.

All: **Amen.**

THE WORD

ASSURANCE

Leader: Hear the word to us in Christ:
'I will never leave you nor forsake you
until the end of time'.

People: **Thanks be to God.**

AFFIRMATION OF FAITH

All: **We believe that we are truly the children of God,
even us,
who hardly dare to say that name,
who joke in our most serious times
and laugh because we know
a moment is important.
Even us,
who are the sons and daughters
of many places and people,
who hardly dare to think of our beginnings
except to know
that we are the ones who somehow survived
and we will not give respect undeserved
to those who think they have a right to be respected.**

**We believe that now and then
we see a greater hope, a greater dream
than we have seen before.
In that dream we are indeed**

**the great south land of the Holy Spirit
where people live equal and free,
where people stand in grace
before each other and their God.
With hope and fragile faith,
we stand before that dream,
our dream
and the dream of God.**

PRAYERS OF INTERCESSION

Leader: Come to us,
as the One who walks the way of ordinary people.

People: **Come to us,
as the One who weeps over the city.**

Leader: Come to us,
as the One who deeply understands
the paradox of life which rises from death.

People: **Come to us,
in a language of grace
that we may approach you
in vulnerable hope.**

Leader: Give us new life,
if the old has been destroyed in us.

People: **Give us openness,
if we have closed our hearts to your future.**

Leader: Give us courage, if we tread this land
in fear of bringing our gifts.

People: **Give us wisdom, when we forget to listen
to the learnings of our history.**

Leader: Give us joy
when we see the breadth of your imagination
expressed in the differences between us.

People: **Differences of race and culture,
differences of history and journey,
differences in our experience of you.**

Leader: Bind us together as those
who feel your love under our feet
in the warmth of this, our holy ground.

People: **Dance within our life, O Spirit of God,
that we may be transformed by your eternal passion
for making all things new.
Amen.**

SONG

BLESSING

Leader: Go in peace
to claim the life of Christ within our midst:
and may the earth be warm under your feet,
the rain bring the gentle flowers of the bush bright
around you
and the wind blow as the breath of the Spirit before you.

All: **Amen.**

LITURGY FOR PRAYER
(AND SO WE PRAY)
For those who don't always find it easy to pray

OPENING SENTENCES

Leader: Pray with us, God who is our loving parent.

People: **Take our hands in yours
and place our feet upon the rock of your faithfulness.**

Leader: Pray with us, Jesus Christ.

People: **Enter the depths of our souls
and know the cry of our hearts on the journey.**

Leader: Pray for us, Holy Spirit.

People: **Find the words for our longings and cover us gently
with your warm, bright wings.
Amen.**

SONG

SHARING OUR HUMANNESS

Leader: Of course we want to pray, O God.
Of course we want to be your people of faith.
But we turn away, for many reasons.
We are silent in our fear, our weakness, our doubt
and we find it hard to believe
in the constancy of your grace.
We share with you now, some of the things
which stop us praying:

(The people share.)

Leader: Take from us, O God,
all the things which separate us from you.

All: *(Sung twice)*
'O Lord, hear our prayer' *(Taizé)*

THE WORD

Romans 8:22-27

AFFIRMATION OF FAITH

All: **We believe in God
who does not leave us alone,
who breathes within our life
and walks within our way.**

**We believe in Jesus Christ
who bears within himself
the great encounter between the demonic and divine,
who stands free within that struggle,
our struggle,
who turns his face towards us all
in eternal grace and costly love.**

**We believe in the Holy Spirit,
who liberates the universe
as it groans in wordless longing
for life that is just and true,
who weeps within our tears
and touches our faces
with the warmth of hope.**

PRAYERS OF INTERCESSION

Leader: We approach you with reverence, O God.
We approach you with honest faith,
sometimes honestly fragile faith or almost none,
sometimes faith which is strong and clear.

People: **These are our prayers,
the prayers of our hearts for those we love,
for the church and the world:**

Leader: They arise in our hearts
like a bird taking wing
and moving towards its Maker.

*(The people bring their prayers as they hold a
small toy bird *and remember their longings.)*

---

*The holding of the bird is important. It seems to help people to pray with honesty and vulnerability. Souvenir and bric-a-brac type gift shops often have small light realistic type birds that feel soft to hold.

Leader: Receive these our prayers, gracious God.

People: **For we pray them in the name of Jesus, the Christ. Amen.**

SONG

BLESSING

Leader: Go forward into this day in peace.
Take up your life in faith.
And may all that you offer to this moment
be expanded and renewed by the love of God,
the courage of Christ
and the freedom of the Holy Spirit.

All: **Amen.**

MISSION:
THE HOLY GROUND OF GOD

GREETING

Leader: The peace of Christ be with you.

People: **And also with you.**

OPENING SENTENCES

Leader: The field of mission:

People: **is the holy ground of God.**

Leader: We tread this way with awe:

People: **in the mystery of grace.**

Leader: For walk we must, even in the silences:

People: **following the call of the Christ.**

SONG

CONFESSION

Voice 1: We hear your voice, O Christ,
saying 'Whom will I send?'
and there is a longing in our hearts
to say 'Send us.'
But we have made so many mistakes
in our ignorance,
in our arrogance,
in our dividedness,
even in our enthusiasm
and we wonder whether
we should stand in silence on this,
your holy ground.

(silent reflection)

Voice 2: We have been saying so many things
for so many years, without much changing
and we wonder whether
we should stand in silence,
on this, your holy ground

| | and stop our speaking,
and our writing
and our meetings. |
|---|---|

(silent reflection)

Voice 3: We have been working so hard,
for so long
with small energies and few resources
and, when others rush past us without speaking
as though they will carry the Gospel
beyond us and without us,
we wonder whether
we should stand in silence,
on this, your holy ground
and close our circle behind them.

(silent reflection)

Leader: Jesus, remember us and forgive us.

All: *(Sung twice)*
'Jesus, remember us, when you come into your kingdom.'
(Taizé)

ASSURANCE

Leader: Hear the word of God for us:
'I, the Lord, have called you in righteousness
and will hold your hand.
I will keep you
and give you as a covenant to the people.
Behold, the former things have come to pass
and new things I declare.
Before they spring forth,
I announce them to you.'

People: **Thanks be to God!**

All: *(Sung)*
'Santo, Santo, Santo' *(World Council of Churches)*

READINGS

REFLECTION ON THE WORD

AFFIRMATION OF FAITH

Leader: In response to the Word, let us stand
and affirm our faith:

All: We believe in light beyond our seeing,
flowing forth
from the flame of life in God
who goes on creating in us
down through the ages of ages.

We believe in healing beyond our knowing,
from the Christ
whose robe stands close
to the reach of our hand
and the pain of our struggle
beyond the end of time.

We believe in the energy of God's Spirit,
stirring in our being
with a rhythm of courage and passion,
moving our feet
to risk Christ's way again
as those who are always called to be
the humble, human witnesses
to the faithfulness of God.

INTERCESSION

Leader: Mission belongs to you, O God.
The ground is holy
because you are already there.
All we are and all we do in faith
is dependent on you
and the victory already won.
We place ourselves in your hands again
and ask for all that we need to do the task.

(The people name the gifts they need.)

Leader: We gather in our midst
those who are our partners in the task
and place them in your hands, loving God.

(The people name their friends.)

Leader: Into our emptiness:

People: **breathe your fullness.**

Leader: Into our tiredness:

People: **pour your energy.**

Leader: If we are discouraged:

People: **bring us your hope.**

Leader: If we are afraid:

People: **bring us your courage.**

Leader: If we do not know the way:

People: **give to us your wisdom.
For we are your people
and you are our God,
forever and forever.
Amen.**

Leader: And now we pray your prayer as one:

People: **Our Father . . .**

SONG

BLESSING

Leader: Go into this day,
with a lifting of the heart.
And may the Triune God
be in our beginnings,
and endings,
and the journey in between.

All: **Amen.**

LITURGY FOR EASTER 1

WE GATHER

Leader: We gather again this Easter
at the foot of the cross
which calls us on,
not in shame,
not in fear,
but more deeply into the costly journey
towards life.
There is wounding, there is weeping.
In Jesus Christ,
God is not separated from that.

CALL TO WORSHIP

Leader: In the shadow of our suffering:

People: **is the suffering of Jesus.**

Leader: In the shadow of our weakness:

People: **is the vulnerability of the Christ.**

Leader: In the shadow of our pain:

People: **is the God who cried out.**

Leader: We are never rejected,

People: **we are called on to abundant life.**

HYMN

MOVING CLOSER TOWARDS OURSELVES
First Reading: Luke 23:1-32

Leader: God in Christ, you travel with us in faith
towards the hard places in our souls.
You know the agony of pain, guilt and hurt
deep within us.
You know our frightened faces,
often hidden from ourselves.
You know the violence sometimes hurled in anger
because we feel powerless to take
the smallest steps to freedom.

You know the grief lying there,
embalmed and perfumed
by our resolve to remain victims forever.

There are stumbling blocks within ourselves
in our travelling, O God.
We take these stones, these hard things in our lives,
and lay them at the foot of the cross
which is able to bear the weight and wounding for us.

*(Silent reflection on the hard things want to lay
at the foot of the cross)*

Leader: We leave these hard things here?
on our way through to life.

All: *(Sung)*
'Bless the Lord, my soul. . .' *(Taizé)*

Reader : Luke 23: 33-48

'Then all his friends stood at a distance, and they saw all this happen.'

(The cross is lifted and held before the people.)

'When it was evening, there came a rich man of Arimathea, called Joseph, who had become a disciple of Jesus. He went to Pilate and asked for the body of Jesus: it was handed over to him.'

(The shroud is placed on the floor.)

'Joseph took the body, wrapped it in a clean shroud, and put it in his own new tomb which he had hewn out of the rock.'

(The cross is placed on the shroud.)

All: *(Sung)*
'Bless the Lord my soul. . .'

REFLECTION

Reader: 'Near the cross of Jesus stood his mother and his mother's sister, Mary the wife of Clopas and Mary of Magdala. Many women were there watching from a distance. Among them were the mother of Zebedee's sons, and Joanna, and Mary the mother of James and Joseph.

	These women, who had travelled with Jesus from Galilee and looked after him, were following behind.'
Leader:	Mary watched the death of her innocent child and held him in her arms.

(Flowers are placed on the cross.)

Leader:	We remember the death of our innocent selves. We remember the death of innocent fragile things in the world around us.

(Silent reflection)

Leader:	It is time to leave this place. Jesus said 'Father, into your hands, I commit my spirit'.
All:	'Bless the Lord, my soul …' *(Taizé)*

AFFIRMATION OF FAITH

Leader:	As we also commend ourselves into the hands of God, let us say what we believe:
All:	**We believe that we are safe in the hands of a God who walked into our deaths carrying all the real experience of our being.**
	We believe in this God who truly lived as we do because he cried out with our cry, he was alone with our loneliness and betrayed with our betrayals.
	We believe that we are not defined by the deaths that others deal us, we are not determined by the ways which others name us, and we need not be defeated by the powers which stand against us.
	We claim this peace in Christ. We receive this miracle from our Maker and the Spirit will be our hope even when we do not see it.

HYMN

BLESSING AND DISMISSAL

Leader: Go in peace to love and serve the Christ.

People: **In the name of Christ,
Amen.**

Leader: And may the God of hope be your light,
the God of love be your company
and the God of the Spirit rise in truth before you.

All: **Amen.**

LITURGY FOR EASTER 2
A journey from Good Friday to Easter Day

GREETING
Leader: Christ be with you!

People: **And also with you.**

CELEBRATE THE SEEDS OF LIFE
Leader: Celebrate the seeds of life which lie within us.

People: **Let us carry them on the way of the cross and safely into risen life in Christ.**

Leader: For God is with us,
around us and within us.

People: **Life and love are stronger than death. Thanks be to God!**

SONG

ENTRY INTO DEATH
Leader: 'Except a grain of wheat falls into the ground and dies, it remains alone. But if it dies, it bears much fruit.'
The passion of Christ,
the journey into Good Friday,
is an invitation to take the seed of life which is ours
and allow it to enter the darkness of its inner life
and the earthy darkness of the world around it.
Here we may safely face our pain and weakness,
our failure and griefs,
our woundedness and our woundings.
Here, as we entrust that fragile seed to Jesus Christ,
we will be held by One
who can receive all our reality
with understanding, grace and costly love.
Let us look at the wheat seed in our hands
and, in the quiet,
dare to know who we are before God.

(silent reflection)

Leader: Guard us on this journey, O Christ.

People **Keep us safe as we follow you in faith.**

ASSURANCE

Leader: Nothing in heaven or on earth
can separate us from the love of God in Christ Jesus.
God forgives us, heals us and brings us to life.

All: **Amen.**

(Sung) 'Bless the Lord my soul and bless God's holy name' *(Taizé)*

(repeat twice)

READINGS

(followed by silent reflection)

AFFIRMATION OF FAITH

Leader: In response to the word, let us stand and affirm our faith:

All: **We believe in God,
who when there was nothing
planted the seeds of life in all creation,
green in the desert,
gold in the wattle trees
and breath in the clay of human life.**

**We believe in Jesus Christ,
eternal seed of life
who entered the deaths of our existence,
trod deeply into our earthiness,
took into his body all our painfulness
and lifted it into the victory of love.**

**We believe in the Holy Spirit
who waters our grief with her tears,
nourishes in us the buds of life,
and tenderly cherishes our growings
until they break forth
into the fruits of hope and faith.**

INTERCESSION

Leader: As we look at ourselves, the church and the world, let us see the signs of the seeds of new life, however small.
Take a seed from the basket,
place it on Christ's table where seeds are turned into bread,
and name the sign you see or the hope you have:

(The people place the seeds.)

O God, we are never without your hope of newness,

People: **We pray that you will take these fragile signs,
seeds of our longing,
and bring them to abundant life.
Amen.**

THE EUCHARIST

THE SETTING OF THE TABLE

Leader: This table stands among us,
Christ's table and our table

People: **We gather around it
in our common humanness,
one people in our frailty
none more worthy than the other,
all made worthy in the resurrection of Christ.**

Leader: The seeds of our life are joined on the table
with the life of Christ.

People: **With joy we bring the gifts of bread and wine;
in faith we name this our holy table
as it carries the Body of Christ.**

THE EUCHARIST CONTINUES. . .

SONG

DISMISSAL AND BLESSING

Leader: As you brought with you the seed in your hand
so believe that it always lies within you.
As you have received the life of Christ,
so take these small loaves
as the sign of the work of the Spirit in your midst
bringing forth the fruits of grace.

(The loaves are passed around.)

Leader: Go in peace, for Christ is risen!

People: **Christ is risen indeed!**
Amen.

The Journey in Between

*In the Spirit of joy and dreams
we live on in the face of the struggle,
laughing and weeping
in the centre of our pain,
celebrating in the power of our solidarity
with all who stand for love and hope
and the victory of right.*

HOLD YOUR HEADS HIGH
OUR LIBERATION IS AT HAND

OPENING SENTENCES

Leader: Lift up your hearts!

People: **We are warmed by our hope in Christ.**

Leader: Lift up your voices!

People: **For even the stones cry out.**

Leader: Lift up your heads!

People: **Our freedom is near at hand.
Thanks be to God.**

HYMN

THIS IS WHO WE ARE

Leader: As we know your nearness, O God,
we know more clearly who we are.
We are your people who struggle with many things.
We see your reign at hand,
but it still seems beyond our reach.
In these things it seems far away:

(The people share the struggles in their life and work.)

At intervals the leader will say:

Leader: O Christ, hear our prayer

People: **Be with us we struggle, O God.**

(or/and appropriate sung response)

ASSURANCE

Leader: There is no time or place
which is far from the love of God.
Hold your heads high.
Our liberation is at hand!

All: **Amen.**

THE WORD Luke 21: 25-33

THE SIGNS OF THE REIGN OF GOD

Leader: In thankfulness,
we celebrate the signs of the sovereignty of God,
which we have found in our life and work together here.

(The people light a candle and name the sign.)

Leader: In faith, we join these our signs with those of our sisters and brothers around the world.

(silent reflection)

Leader: With an awareness of our unique place in the eternal plan of God, we remember some of those who have gone before us: *(The people name those who have been their inspiration.)* and all who will come after us.

(silent reflection)

Leader: We are not alone.

People: **We stand in a great company, with the whole communion of saints.**

Leader: They have prepared the way:

People: **And so will we, by the grace of God. Amen.**

Leader: In us will the flowering of the Spirit be seen.
In each one,
Christ will call forth a blossoming of new things.
The peace of Christ be with you.

People: **And also with you.**

(The people write the names of these people on a cloth which is placed on the table.)

HYMN

COMMISSIONING AND BLESSING

Leader: Take up the task with hope and faith!

People: **We believe that we are the children of God.**

Leader: The world is always waiting for us to emerge:
so, go with courage into the costly path of Christ,
go with imagination into the creative life of God
and go with freedom into the life of the Spirit.

All: **Amen.**

For my friend, Brian Wren, hymn writer for those who want to begin with vulnerability and end with hope and faith together.

CARRIERS OF A HOPE
A service for people who work together

OPENING SENTENCES

Leader: We are those who try to carry a hope into being,

People: **A hope that we might work together
in true community.**

Leader: We are those who try to carry a task,

People: **A task that, here and there,
might bring a little more life to the world.**

Leader: We have not yet come near to our vision for ourselves
and the world,

People: **But we hold to the hope that is ours.**

LIGHTING OF THE CANDLE

Leader: There is an old saying:
'It is better to light a candle than to curse the darkness.'
We light this candle, a light for our journey.
For some of us, it is the sign of the light of Christ.

(The candle is lit.)

OFTEN WE ARE TIRED

Leader: Those who carry the weight,
the weight of good and worthy things
and the weight of less than worthy things in our life,
become tired of the carrying.
Hold the stone in your hand.
What are you carrying that you would like to lay down?

(The basket is passed from person to person and each one is invited to place the stone in the basket, either in silence or to share what that person would like to lay down. The basket is then placed in the centre.)

Leader: Let us reflect on the burdens that lie in our lives.
Let us honour the tiredness, pain, anger and woundedness
that lies among us, shared and unshared.

(silent reflection)

O God, only you know the truth of the burden
which each of us carries.
We know that some of the burdens
which we wish to lay down
can be picked up by the gifts and energy of others.
Sometimes we can be so supported by others
that the things we are carrying seem lighter.
Sometimes we can change our life in ways
which bring new justice and care.
For other things, we have few answers,
too few resources in ourselves
to bring in the changes,
or we simply fail in what we would hope to do or be.

People: **For this we grieve.**
For this we pray forgiveness.
For all, we pray for new ways
to journey on in hope.
Amen.

THE WORD

Some options: Isaiah 65:17-23a; Isaiah 55:10-13; Isaiah 46:3 and 4; Isaiah 40:1-5; Isaiah 42:5-9; Ephesians 1:15-19; Revelation 21:1-6.

CELEBRATION OF THE CARRYING

Leader: Let us share with each other
those things in our work which we enjoy carrying.
Let us pass the basket to each other
and choose a good thing to represent the things we celebrate
in our work together.

(The basket of flowers, herbs and sweets is passed around the circle and each person shares one thing that they celebrate in their work.)

AFFIRMING OUR HOPE

Leader: Let us affirm what is there
and commit ourselves to go on in the journey together:

Voice 1: We affirm the...*(any activities which unite and encourage people)*

Voice 2: We affirm the projects we are planning
and the opportunities for review and assessment,
when we try to negotiate better
for our hope and expectations.

Voice 3: We affirm the multitudes of moments
in churches, corridors, lifts, offices and coffee shops,
when we discover we have friends and colleagues,
when there are moments of honesty, of creative conflict
and networking which lead us on.

People: **We affirm these things in our midst.
Make more of them, O God.
Take them on beyond where we have yet been.
In faith, we make our commitment
to each other.
In hope, we will go on.
Amen.**

PRAYERS FOR OUR WORK

Leader: Before God, we remember each section of our work
and place it in God's hands for cherishing,
for healing, for wisdom, for creativity, for energy
and for liberation to new life.

*(Each section of work is named with time for silent prayer
or reflection after each naming.)*

We remember:

(The sections of work are named.)

Leader: For all this work and for ourselves,
the carriers of the load and the carriers of the hope,

People: **We pray in faith, O God.
Amen.**

SENDING OUT

Leader: Go in peace.
Go as the people of the feast.

People: **Called to share in the breaking of the bread,
called to share in common life.**

Leader: And may God the Creator go on creating in us;
the God in Christ walk with us in our humanness
and the Holy Spirit dance before us in new freedom.

All: **Amen.**

THE FEAST OF GOD
Agape Meal

The people gather for the meal.

GREETING

Leader: The peace of Christ be with you

People: **And also with you.**

OPENING SENTENCES

Leader: We are the people of the feast of God.

People: **The feast which feeds the hungry, body, mind, heart and soul.
The feast which pours the water of life into the thirsty depths of our being.**

Leader: We are those who are offered life in all its fullness.

People: **Life to be shared in justice, freedom and peace.**

Leader: In thanksgiving we gather.

People: **The feast is for all.**

SONG

The meal begins.

After a period the leader invites the people to 'gather' others into the feast as follows:

THE GATHERING IS NOT FINISHED

Leader: The gathering of God is for all who will come.
The celebration is for a hope that is already won in Jesus Christ.
But we are not all here.
The hope of Jesus Christ is not yet complete in us.
Who do we long to gather into our community?

The people name people and groups who they long to invite into the feast of God.

After each naming, a small candle is lit at the table where each speaker is seated.

Leader: Gather all these we have named into our midst, O God.
Place them in our hearts and prayers,
place them in our working and struggling
to bring the whole world under your reign of love.

People: **In faith, and in your name, O God,
we gather these, our sisters and brothers,
into our feast.
Amen.**

THE ASSURANCE

Leader: In Jesus Christ, even as we live in our brokenness,
we are called to be the guests at the table,
freed from the things that separate us
from each other and from God.
Come, eat, drink.
In faith, we are restored to the household of God.

All: **Thanks be to God!**

The meal goes on for a period.

THE WORD

Readings

*Stories of celebration, or moments of achievement
and hope are shared.*

After the stories:

Leader: The living Word is among us,
even among us, who are ordinary human people

People: **The light of Christ is in our midst.
Thanks be to God!**

A larger candle is lit on each table.

THE AFFIRMATION OF FAITH

Leader: In response to the word, let us stand and affirm our faith:

All: **We are made in the image of God,
echoes of the Creator,
children of a loving energy,
one with the universe and all that lies within it.**

**Christ has been born in our earthiness,
seen in the face of justice,**

vivid in our moments of truth,
dying and living in the passion of our life.

We can feel the power of the Spirit,
surrounding us with grace.
She is wise in the centre of our wanderings,
and joyfully gathering the whole creation
into the freedom of God.

This we believe.
This we affirm.
From this we will live.

The meal proceeds until shortly before the end.

WE ARE TOGETHER

Leader: We are not alone.
We share the task and we share the nurturing gifts of God.
We share the common humanness
and we share the common hope in Christ.
Let us stand.
As we leave this place let us offer to each other
a glass of water from the jug in the centre of each table.

People: **In this water lie the tears
we share along the way.
They will be transformed
into the water of life for us all.**

Each person gives a glass of water to the person on their left with the words 'May this be the water of life for you'.

Leader: Let us pray:
Come close to where we stand, Jesus Christ.
Bring the hem of your robe against our fingers
that we may be healed, restored,
and filled with the energy and courage of your life.

People: **Come close to us, Jesus Christ,
hope of the world.**

Leader: Lay your hands on the world, O God.
Anoint it with your costly love.
If it is poor:

People: **Flood it with your generous gifts.**

Leader: If it is oppressed:

People: **Break its chains of bondage,
turn them into barriers
to keep the people safe.**

Leader: If it grieves:

People: **Show it the face of your weeping
and the comfort of your Spirit.**

Leader: Go with us into the world, O God,

People: **That we may be your people,
as you are our God.
Amen.**

SONG

COMMISSIONING AND BLESSING

Leader: Go in peace to love and serve the Christ and the world.
And may God the Creator go on creating within us,
God in Jesus Christ sit at table in our midst
and the Spirit lead us in the dance of life.

All: **Amen.**

The people pass the peace with each other as they go.

THE GOLDEN ONES
A Eucharist for people who feel marginalised

GREETING
Leader: The peace of Christ be with you.

People: **And also with you.**

OPENING SENTENCES
Leader: We are the golden children of God:

People: **Lying below the surface of life's earth
in hidden beauty and value.**

Leader: We wait to be discovered:

People: **As the Divine waits in everyone,
full of loving humanness.**

Leader: In us the Spirit dances and sings:

People: **found in the melody of possible music
which hums and moves in all creation.
Thanks be to God!**

SONG

IT'S NOT EASY
Leader: It's not easy being who we are, O God.
We often wonder what you are doing,
not because we have problems about being who we are
but because others do.
They have so much power to take life from us,
create so much fear in us
that the claiming of our life
becomes an endless act of courage.

We are tired of hiding ourselves
and explaining ourselves
and limiting ourselves, O God.
We do not wish to deny ourselves any longer
because it destroys the wholeness to which we are called.

People: **Free us to life, to love and justice,
O God who made us.**

ASSURANCE

Leader: In Christ, we share the road with the one
who wept over Jerusalem,
and walked towards the oppressors there
with costly hope and trembling faith.

All: **Amen.**

THE WORD

(followed by silent reflection)

AFFIRMATION OF FAITH

Leader: In response to the word, let us affirm our faith:

All: **In the God of all creation,
we have our life and being,
children of divine imagination
born from love,
for freedom and for truth
and human being.**

**In the God in Christ,
we see the vision for our journeying,
walking unknown paths
through crucifixions and resurrections,
treading past our bleeding
with passionate hearts
into small spaces where life is reborn.**

**In the Spirit of joy and dreams
we live on in the face of the struggle,
laughing and weeping
in the centre of our pain,
celebrating in the power of our solidarity
with all who stand for love and hope
and the victory of right.**

WE NEED HELP

Leader: Let us light a candle for those we trust to be our support
in this journey:

(The people say the names and light candles.)
And God will be our help
in this time of struggle,
in the days and nights of our fearfulness
and need for courage.

People: **We hope for energy and wisdom,
for resources of strength,
for companions when the way is lonely
and for a sense that we are indeed
the children of good.**

Leader: We pray for all who are rejected and patronised,
all who have suffered at the hands of the church
when it betrays its God.
Give to them comfort and certainty
in their determination to live.
Give to us all these gifts, O God,
for we ask for them in faith.
Amen.

THE EUCHARIST

THE OFFERTORY

THE GREAT THANKSGIVING

Leader: The Lord be with you.

People: **And also with you.**

Leader: Lift up your hearts.

People: **We lift them up to God.**

Leader: Let us give thanks to the Lord our God.

People: **It is right to give our thanks and praise.**

Leader: Holy God, we praise and thank you
for all the creativity we find in ourselves
and for your respecting of the struggles of your creation,
even our struggles,
and for the ripples of your grace
which flow forth eternally in all that is.
We thank you for Jesus Christ,
who walked within all of our reality,
stood in the centre of our betrayals,
and with all integrity
claimed the glory of life,
hard won, and coloured deep
with the blood of our pain.
God in the torn apart.
God in the wholeness,
God in the emptiness,

*God in the fullnesses
you are always God with us.
And so we praise you...*

THE INSTITUTION

THE MEMORIAL PRAYER

Leader: As we break this bread
and share this wine:

People: **we receive a God
who is at the centre of our brokenness
and the brokenness of the world,
and we drink a cup
which we all hold in common.**

Leader: As we wait in faith
for the healing love of Christ,

People: **we sing of a dream of reborn hope
and the power of love.**

THE EUCHARIST CONTINUES ...

THANKSGIVING AFTER COMMUNION

Leader: Let us pray:

All: **We thank you, gracious God,
that we are the guests at your table.
As we have been fed by your gifts of life,
so we will share with the world
all that you give to us in love.
Amen.**

SONG

COMMISSIONING AND BLESSING

Leader: Take up the task with hope and faith!

People: **We believe that we are the children of God.**

Leader: The world is always waiting for us to emerge:
so, go with courage into the costly path of Christ,
go with imagination into the creative life of God
and go with freedom into the life of the Spirit.

All: **Amen.**

HONOUR GOD WITH YOUR OFFERING

OPENING SENTENCES

Leader: God sets us free:
People: **Calls us in love to the fullness of life.**
Leader: Christ respects our humanness:
People: **Walks with us in all our struggles.**
Leader: The Spirit celebrates our moving forward:
People: **Dances ahead of us, leading us on.**
All: **Let us worship God!**

HYMN

IT'S NOT EASY

Leader: O God, you know it is not always easy for us
to honour you.
Our future feels insecure
and we feel the need to hold what we have.
There are many calls on our money
and we worry about our decisions.
We don't always trust each other, or the church,
to use our gifts wisely,
and we are tempted so often to buy things
to fill the empty spaces in our lives.
(silent reflection)
God of grace, forgive us.
People: **Forgive us and set us free
to be the people we long to be.**

THE ASSURANCE OF PARDON

Leader: Hear the word to us in Jesus Christ.
There is no condemnation for those who believe.
Rise up and live in freedom and hope!
People: **Thanks be to God.**

THE WORD

Readings

HYMN

SERMON

AFFIRMATION OF FAITH

Leader: In response to the word, let us stand and affirm our faith:

All: **We believe in God,
who trusts us with the whole creation,
who calls us to honour that trust
by living in fairness, justice
generosity and grace.**

**We believe in Jesus Christ,
who walked the way of the cross
to honour God's love for us,
who shared all our struggles
and lived our deepest fears.**

**We believe in the Holy Spirit
who is present in our inner longings,
stirring us into new things,
calling us to the risks of faith.**

PRAYERS OF THANKSGIVING
AND INTERCESSION

Leader: We thank you, God, that your love for us is free,
that you offer us the dignity of decision-making
and respect the choices we make.

People: **We thank you that you are with us
in anger and pain
and with us in joy and celebration.**

Leader: We thank you that you give to us
dreams and visions for our future
and the future of the world which you love,
dreams of being more just, more sharing,
less dependent on things and
living in closer community
with each other and the world.
In these moments of silence,
we wait for your voice to us:

(silent reflection)

Leader: Let us come forward and light a small candle
as a sign of each new possibility for honouring God.
Share the new hope with everyone as you do this,
or light the candle in silence before God.

(The people come forward.)

Leader: Take our hopes and dreams, O God;
honour them with your power to change us.

People: **Give us the warm heart of Hannah
who offered you what she loved the most.
Give us the faith of your witnesses down the ages
that we may worship you in spirit and in truth.
Amen.**

OFFERING

Leader: Let us bring our offerings in honour to God.

(The offering is received.)

DEDICATION

Leader: O God, we believe that you receive our gifts,
knowing what they cost us,
knowing where we are in our journey with you.

People: **We give them with grateful hearts
and invite you to call us on in faith.
Amen.**

HYMN

BLESSING AND DISMISSAL

Leader: Go in peace,
loved and honoured of God.
And may yours be a journey of thanksgiving
lifted up on the winds of the Spirit,
on fire with the passion of Jesus Christ
and held fast in the gentleness of God.

All: **Amen.**

SERVICE FOR HEALING
For a group of people who feel wounded or betrayed

GREETING
Leader: Christ be with you

People: **And also with you.**

OPENING SENTENCES
Leader: Our God is a God who longs to be with us

People: **Who reaches into our deepest places
who weeps within our tears.**

Leader: Our God is a God who holds us
in the womb-space of compassion

People: **Labouring to bring us to birth
in the new life of freedom,
tasting the blood of our pain.**

Leader: Our God is like a rock

People: **Unmoved from love,
unshaken by the anger in our righteous protest
firm beneath our feet
in the eternal creating of our holy ground.**

THE GRIEVING JOURNEY
Leader: Let us recall the journey of grieving,
the place of safety and joy which has been left
and the loss along the way:

(The grievings, losses and disappointments are named.)

Leader: Let us taste the tears in this journey we have had together:

(The bowl of tears is shared and the pain honoured in silence.)

THE WORD
Readings

Silent reflection

THE AFFIRMATION

All: **There is no death
from which you cannot rise in us,
O God.
The power to fail
can never kill the gift of life,
unless we choose
not to receive it from you.
Your Spirit is never defeated
by the woundings of life
however unjust,
however painful.
Your grace in Christ
goes well beyond our understanding
and your love for us
is never measured
by our love for ourselves.
Even as we walk a hard journey
we will claim together
this great hope.
Amen.**

PRAYERS OF INTERCESSION

Leader: Let us place in the hands of God,
all that disturbs us,
all our longings for those whom we hold
in loving concern:

(The people share their prayers.)

Leader: O Lord, hear our prayer.

All: *(Sung)*
**O Lord, hear our prayer, O Lord, hear our prayer.
When we pray, answer us,
O Lord, hear our prayer, O Lord, hear our prayer,
come and listen to us.**
(Repeat)

THE ANOINTING

Leader: In the name of the Christ,
who has walked every journey before you
and sees deeply into your heart in understanding,
we announce a new day.
Receive the grace of God
and the healing of the Holy Spirit,
in the name of Christ,

All: **Amen.**

(The people pass to each other a pot of fragrant oil and anoint each other on the hand or forehead with the words 'Receive the grace of God.')

SONG

BLESSING

Leader: Go in peace.
And may the God of grace encircle your soul
the God in Christ reach out to touch you
and the Spirit shine light on your path.

All: **Amen.**

This service can be adapted for a service which focuses on personal healing.

WE ARE THE ONES WHO ARE LOVED
A celebration of our freedom to play

GREETING
Leader: The Lord be with you.

People: **And also with you.**

CALL TO WORSHIP
Leader: God, who gave us the creation to play in,
with rolling landscapes of delight,
with wonders of earth and sea
and endless discoveries of beauty:

People: **We worship you.**

Leader: God who made us in infinite diversity,
with all the vivid colours of our differences,
all the magic of our unknowns
to be explored and celebrated:

People: **We worship you.**

Leader: God, who in your being
carries the One who loved to feast with friends,
who sat in silence on the mountain tops alone,
whose Spirit dances in all the earth:

People: **We worship you
in Spirit and in truth.**

HYMN

CONFESSION
Leader: O God, if we have taken your gifts for granted
and exploited them or used more than our due:

People: **Forgive us.**

Leader: If we have chosen to live driven lives,
refusing to stop and receive your peace and rest,
rushing past the delights you planned for our healing:

People: **Forgive us.**

(Silent reflection)

Leader: If we have failed to receive with hospitality
the strangers among us
who are never strange to you:

People: **Forgive us and open our hearts to your grace.**

ASSURANCE OF PARDON

Leader: The grace of God is infinite and free.
Rise up and live with faith and hope.

THE WORD

All: **From the Spirit have we all received,
grace upon grace.**

Readings: Psalm 65, Luke 15:11-32

AFFIRMATION OF FAITH

Leader: In response to the Word, let us affirm our faith:
Life is a litany of love,
ringing in the moment of our birth,
sounding clear in the centre of our labouring,
called again and again into joy.

People: **And we are the ones who are loved.
Thanks be to God.**

Leader: The rhythm of love ripples on
transforming our innocence into wisdom,
gasping into life again
as we survive the waves of harsh moments.

People: **And we are the ones who are loved.
Thanks be to God.**

Leader; We are the ones who are loved,
surrounded by countless gracious signs,
cherished in the gentle hands of God,

All: **This we believe,
from this we will live.
Thanks be to you, Jesus Christ.**

INTERCESSION

Leader: Let us pray for our ministry,
lighting a small candle for each place:
(The people light the candles and name the place.)
Into your hands we give these ministries, O God;
inspire them with your Holy Spirit.

People: **Take our gifts
and turn them into baskets
of overflowing grace.**

Leader: Teach us to play, to rest, to be the people of the feast,
that we may be the ones of abundant life:

People: **filled to overflowing
with the generosity of your life,
living with lightness of being,
delighting in the colour, music, dancing
and passion of the creation.
Amen.**

SONG

BLESSING AND SENDING OUT

Leader: Go in faith, for there is God,
riding in the light on the water,
singing in the songs of the birds,
sitting in the midst of the parties of life.

People: **We go in faith
to live in joyous freedom,
to play in the creation
and to drink deeply of the gracious cup of life.
Amen.**

WASH OUR FEET

OPENING SENTENCES

Leader: And as they sat around a table,
as the friends of Jesus,
Jesus took a basin and a towel
and began to wash their feet.

People: **This our God,
the one who knew
that all things were given into his hands.**

SONG

BUT WE DON'T ALWAYS WANT YOU TO WASH OUR FEET

Leader: Jesus, we don't always want you to wash our feet.
We would rather have a God who keeps at a distance,
full of majesty and mystery,
clothed in white upon a mountain top or cloud.

People: **Our feet are too close to the mud under them,
the ordinary earthiness of our life.**

Leader: Jesus, our feet are not often the best part of us.
We would rather you washed our hearts
or maybe our souls,
preferably on one of our better days.

People: **Our feet are very vulnerable, Jesus,
to where we have been
and what we have done.**

Leader: Jesus, maybe you could wash our faces.
We try our best to make them beautiful for other people
and they are usually rather clean
and we could smile at you as you wash us.

People: **Feet are so very closed in
and worn with the weight of our carrying.
Washing of feet brings you very near to us as you kneel
so we could reach and touch your face.**

ASSURANCE

Leader: As Jesus washed the feet of his friends,
he became their servant,
the One who knew them as they were,
the One who was like them,
the One who showed them how to be with each other.
The word to us in Christ
is that we need never fear the nearness of the Christ
because that is grace and healing.

All: **Thanks be to God!**

READINGS

AFFIRMATION

Leader: In response to the word, let us affirm our faith:

All: **Our God serves us,
kneels before us and gently holds
our worn and earthy feet,
noting the sorenesses
and harsh-rubbed places
as though they are the woundings
of a journey.**

**Our God washes our feet
as a sharing on the way,
not separated by cosmic distance
or heavenly hosts,
but with head near,
touching our knees
and towel tied around his waist.**

**Our God does not set us down in this place
and watch us as we go,
left alone to run the course of our days,
remarking on our stumblings.
Our God brushes off our dust,
and measures with pride
the miles we have come,
always cherishing us for the new day.**

WE WILL LET YOU SERVE US

Leader: Please do serve us, Jesus Christ.
We are not as strong as we pretend to be
and the way often seems very long.

People: **If we let you serve us, sharing in our life,
we could serve our sisters and brothers
in thanksgiving.**

Leader: Please do wash us, Jesus Christ.
We often feel guilty and far from clean
and it's hard for us to believe
that we will ever be other than that.

People: **If we were made clean,
we might not feel so badly about ourselves
and could see others differently too.**

Leader: Please care for us, Jesus Christ;
we sometimes feel
as though nobody notices that we need loving care
and that you probably don't notice either.

People: **If you care for us,
maybe our hearts would overflow
with generous love for others
and we could take the bowl and towel from you
and find many worn and tired feet
to wash in your name,
Jesus Christ.
This is our prayer for us and the world, gentle God.
Amen.**

SONG

BLESSING

Leader: Go in peace as the loved children of God;
and when the way is rough,
may you feel the touch of the Christ on your feet;
when the way is long,
may the Spirit lift you up
and when the way is hard,
may the hand of God close around you.

All: **Amen.**

... AND THE DANCE GOES ON

GREETING
Leader: Christ be with you.
People: **And also with you.**

OPENING SENTENCES
Leader: We wondered whether we would have the energy:
People: **or the heart for the ongoing.**
Leader: We felt the world, with all its desperation:
People: **and relentless deathly cycles.**
Leader: But, sometimes, for a moment,
it all becomes framed in light beyond our seeing.
In ourselves,
we feel the movement of possible music:
People: **And in the Spirit of God,**
the Spirit of Christ,
the dance goes on.

SONG

STANDING STILL
Leader: Many things paralyse us, O God.
There is despair and fear,
endless struggle for enough resources,
confusion and too many discussions
because we would rather stand still
than make a mistake.
We spend our energy struggling over small things
while the world groans in pain
and the cries of the people are more than we can bear.
We carry the heavy burden of our guilt
while you wait to forgive us and free us
to lightness of soul.
The way seems hard and we are often weary, O God.

(silent reflection and prayer)

We come to you in humble faith:

People: **Forgive us, heal us and free us, O God of grace.**
Come to us because, without you,
the way ahead is too hard for us to tread.
Amen.

ASSURANCE

Leader: *(Holding a small bird)*
As God holds this small bird, in all its vulnerability,
so God holds us and the world in loving care.
Rest in the hands of God for healing
and soon there will be freedom to fly.

People: **Thanks be to God.**

THE WORD

Readings

AFFIRMATION

Leader: In response to the word, let us stand and affirm our faith:

All: **In God,**
our deaths are not the final word,
our moments of crisis
are part of eternal possibility,
and our weakness
is taken up into the courage of God.

In Christ,
our humanness is touched with divine life,
our tears are mingled
with the longing love of Jesus,
and our solidarity with those who suffer
is joined by the divine presence.

In the Spirit,
there are no boundaries on the dream,
there is no end to hope,
there will be a world beyond our seeing
and we will never live
beyond the cherishing of God.

AND WE WILL JOIN THE DANCE

Leader: Sisters and brothers,
in the power of God and the power of our life together,
will we move forward, risking the way of Jesus,
taking up the task of this day and the days to come?

People: **In faith we will accept our calling in Jesus Christ.**
In hope we will be the children of God.
Amen.

SONG

BLESSING AND DISMISSAL

Leader: Go in peace to love and serve the Christ and the world.
And may God the Creator go on creating within us,
God in Jesus Christ sit at table in our midst
and the Spirit lead us in the dance of life.

All: **Amen.**

Endings

*There is a God
who says to us
weep strongly,
be strongly afraid,
care strongly,
choose life strongly in faith
and I will live strongly
in all of that.*

GRIEVING THE CHILD
A service for those whose child has a disability

OPENING SENTENCES

Leader: Carried with love under our heart:

People: **we waited for you.**

Leader: Held close in the depths of our beings:

People: **we waited for you.**

Leader: Born from the life of God:

People: **we imaged this one -
sound of body, mind, heart and soul
small gift of beauty and life.**

THIS WAS NOT TO BE

Leader: But this, our child, faces life with a disability.
In its very beginnings there is placed a struggle
for fullness of life.

It's not really that we weep for ourselves, O God,
although we do weep for ourselves too.
We wanted the best start to life for this child
for its own sake.
We longed for it to have all the options
for growing and being.
Life is usually hard anyway
and we wanted it to have every chance.
When we saw the new reality,
we prayed and we prayed
and you didn't seem to hear us, God.

We also really wanted a God
who would protect all children in their vulnerability
and now we don't know how to see you, God.
We don't know how to understand
what has happened to us and our precious child.
Sometimes we cannot help but wonder
if there is something that we have done

                which has caused this?
                But what sort of God would you be
                that would punish our child
                because of something in us?
                We know that is not the God
                we have known in Jesus.

People: **All this is loss, O God.**
                All this is too much for us, O Jesus Christ.

Leader: In the silence
                let us honour our pain.

                (period of silence)

SIGNS OF THE HONOURING

                (A purple cloth is placed on the table, or on the floor in the centre.)

Leader: This purple is the royal covering of pain
                that lies over our life.
                This pain is beyond the commonplace,
                it has dignity and significance,
                it is to be respected and marked.

People: **We will light a tiny candle**
                the flickering of the hope, the life,
                the remnant of our faith.

                (A tea-candle is lit and placed on the cloth.)

THE WORD

The cry: *Psalm 13*
The assurance: Romans 8:22-27 and 31-39

THE AFFIRMATION

Leader: In response to the word, let us say what we believe:

All: **We believe that,**
                in the face of loss and grief,
                we are free to cry out,
                to protest in righteous anger,
                to respect our own pain.

                We believe that this never goes unheard,
                that it is not lost in the silences
                and pits of our sadness.

We believe it is taken into the heart of our God
who weeps with us,
who walks with us
through every moment that has been
and is to come.

We believe that,
as we bow our heads,
the Spirit covers us with her bright wings,
sorrowing in our sorrow
and lifting our faces to the warmth and love
which waits for us,
cherishing us and giving us strength
for this unknown journey.

We believe in this God who says
'I will be with you,
and that will be enough',
even as we find it hard to believe
it will be enough.
In faith, we will move in to the next part of our life,
carrying close to our heart this new child,
this child in need of special care.

WE WILL NEED HELP

Leader: Those were hard-won statements of faith, O God,
and often we cannot hold to them.
It looks like a long journey ahead
and we will need all the help that we can get.

People: **Please gather the right companions around us
for this journey,
the ones who will carry us
when our feet and souls are tired,
the ones who will have faith for us
if our faith falters.**

(The friends pray their own prayers for the family.)

Leader: In Christ you said to us that if we knock, search and ask,
you will send to us the Holy Spirit, O God.
We are knocking, searching and asking now.
Send your Spirit in power upon us
for healing, faith, courage, endurance, and all that
we need for these next days.

People: **In the name of the Christ,
Amen.**

THE NEW CHILD

Leader: The child we expected is not the child we have.
In this moment let us farewell the old child.

(Period of silence)

If it is appropriate, the child is brought into the centre and surrounded by the people who lay their hands upon her/him.

Leader: Here is the child we have,
the new child,
the precious one that belongs to its parents and to all of us
for sacred safe-keeping all the days of his/her life.

People: **We welcome this child with love.
We will watch over this child
and hold it surely within our community of hope.
The life of this child
is a slender thread of gold among us.**

(A gold thread is placed around the candle.)

SONG

BLESSING

Leader: Go in faith.
And may God the Creator be nearer than breath,
Christ our friend hold your hand
and the Spirit surround you with grace.

All: **Amen.**

This liturgy is for our son, Christopher.

A SIMPLE FUNERAL

OPENING

Leader: Friends,
we have come together
because we loved *(name)*
as *(mother, brother, family, friend etc.)*
Here we will mourn her/him leaving us,
honour her/his life and death,
reverently farewell her/his body
and comfort each other.

We come believing that all human life is valuable,
that the truth and integrity and hopefulness
which resides in each life, lives on.
We come, believing that *(name's)* life,
which we celebrate today
and for which we now experience great loss,
is joined in the eternal continuum of human endeavour
stretching into the past and into the future.

Her/his life was lived in its uniqueness with us
and has now passed into the ultimate community
of human existence.
The gifts and graces which she/he offered
are never lost to us.
The creativity which she/he brought to us
in her/his life and relationships
lies now within our own lives
and travels into the future with us.
(If appropriate) Our lives are more beautiful
because we lived with her/him.

PRAYER
OR SILENT REFLECTION

O God, at this moment,
as we come face to face with death
and our own mortality,
we have many feelings
as well as grief,

and possibly fear for the future.
Please come close to us with your love,
travel with us into this serious moment
and open our hearts to each other.
We ask it in the name of Jesus Christ
who faced his own death and the death of a friend.
Amen.

LORD'S PRAYER

(if appropriate)

READINGS

Traditional and/or contemporary

REFLECTION

None of us knows the whole truth
about what lies beyond death.
Christians believe that as we journey
between life and death,
we are safe in the hands of an infinitely gracious God.
We believe that death invites us into total awareness
and know with truth
whether what we have valued in ourselves
has eternal value.
The God who stands with us at that moment
is the same God who was prepared to die in love
for all humankind,
a God who has entered every struggle of our life with us
and who deeply understands the choices we have made.

TRIBUTE

The things we would like to remember about the person.

The minister moves to the casket and placing a hand on it says:
(Name), all these things and more you have given to us.
We respect your journey through life,
with all of its realities.
We pray that you will travel safely
in this next part of your journey.
Our love goes with you.
Let us pray or reflect in silence on this life
and what it has meant to us:

(silent prayer/reflection)

Thanks be to God for the gifts we have received in this person.
Thanks be to God for a life lived with (courage, honesty, grace, determination - as appropriate).

(If a burial)

We will now accompany you to your final resting place.

(The casket is carried to the grave.)

THE FAREWELL

As we come to the moment of farewell,
part of our grief may be regret
for things done or left undone,
words said, or never said,
or moments that never happened.
This is the time to lay aside all those regrets
and to honour the spirit of *(name)* herself/himself,
who would never want them carried into our future.
Let us receive that gift of generosity from *(name)*
and the forgiveness of God.

(silent reflection)

To love someone is to risk the pain of parting.
Not to love is never to have lived.
The grief which we now experience
is the honouring of our love.
Let us now in a quiet moment
make our farewell to (name).

(silence)

THE COMMITTAL

(If a burial)

And now let us commit her/his body to the earth,
which is welcoming to us at the time of our death.
Ashes to ashes, dust to dust.
In the cycle of life and death the earth is replenished
and life is eternally renewed.

(If a cremation)

And now let us commit her/his body to the elements
which are gentle to us at the time of our death.
Ashes to ashes, dust to dust.

In the cycle of life and death the earth is replenished
and life is eternally renewed.
Go in peace, *(name)*.
Travel safely with our love
into the hands of God.
Amen.

BLESSING AND DISMISSAL

Even as we grieve this loss,
let us commit ourselves to the comfort of those
who miss her/him most
especially *(names)*.

Let us surround them with our love
and pray for the comfort of God.

And now let us go into the world,
glad that we have loved,
free to weep for the one we have lost,
free to hold each other in our human frailty,
empowered to live life to the full *(if appropriate)*
as did *(name)*
and to affirm the hope of human existence.
And may God be our company,
Christ Jesus walk before us
and the Spirit surround us with a cloud of grace.
Amen.

I have often used this service during my ministry because I find that many people are better ministered to by simplicity of liturgical style, most especially if they have little or no connection with the church. I always make it clear that I am a Christian minister but indicate that I believe it is both respectful and self-respecting when the church does not pretend a relationship which is not there. Obviously there are many adaptations to be made according to the honest realities of the person concerned.

IN THE END: THERE IS A PASSION

OPENING SENTENCES

Leader: In the end, there is a passion:

People: **deep in the heart of God.**

Leader: It will not let us go:

People: **even if it travels with us
past the moments of death.**

Leader: It rises again and again
in the eternity of love:

People: **a mystery, a wonder, God undefeated.**

SONG

IT'S OFTEN HARD TO BELIEVE

Leader: It's hard to live with passion, God.
You lived that way,
always honest with yourself and other people,
even your friends,
always determined to take the risk
of living really free,
challenging powerful people,
actually caring about things most of the time
and they killed you.

(silent reflection)

We never come close
to living as passionately as that, God,
but still it feels dangerous much of the time.
What if we make choices about our life
which seem to be the best we can do
and then we see them for what they are, and were,
and can't live with ourselves?
They were passionate decisions, God,
born of our blood, sweat and tears,

and we mostly thought you were in them,
at least a little.

(silent reflection)

Mostly we are just longing to be loved
and so we make our choices towards that.
It's hard for us to do otherwise.
You know that, God.
Some of it's about
wanting to keep what we have,
in power and things,
and maybe add a little more.

(silent reflection)

You understand all that, God who is Jesus.
You have felt all that we feel,
longed for all that we long for.
That's why, some of the time,
we believe that you will forgive us.
Let us ask for the forgiveness of this God.

People: **Forgive us and love us,
make sense of our struggles,
O God of grace.**

THE ASSURANCE

Leader: The assurance in Christ
is that this God loves us with such a passion
that God travels with us into death
and defeats that death forever.
Amen.

People: **Thanks be to God!**

THE WORD

Readings
Reflection

THE AFFIRMATION OF FAITH

Leader: Let us respond to the Word:

All: **Even as we seem to be dying
in weakness,
in fear,**

overwhelmed by all the forces against us,
there are moments when we know
that we will never be determined
by any of that.

There is a God
who says to us
weep strongly,
be strongly afraid,
care strongly,
choose life strongly in faith
and I will live strongly
In all of that.

There is a God
who swings from hill to mountain top,
who stands high in the depths of the pit,
who gasps free of the waters of drowning
and plants the cross-shaped tree
on the very shaking ground
on which we stand
as though our trembling earth
is like a rock.

There is a God
who steps free
of the binding chains around our souls
and calls us in a voice
which always knows our name,
and always knows our pain,
who lifts our feet
as though our life
stands cupped in a saving hand
and cherished forever in a safe place.

CALL US ON

Leader: Call us on to the adventure
of your passionate life, O God.

People: **Carry us past the boundaries,
the near horizons of our small dreams.**

Leader: Paint our world in vivid colours
so that we see
a whole new vision of your possibilities.

People: **Hold the cup of living water to our lips
and breathe into our souls
the life of your Spirit.**

Leader: Pour over us the oil of your anointing,
that we may stand tall
as the royal children of your birthing.

People: **Fill us with a fire
which burns from a flame of truth,
refining our beings
so that we dare to take in our hands
your cross of courage, justice,
hope and love
and plant it abroad in all the earth.
We ask this in the name of the One
who walks this way before us
to the end of time.
Amen.**

SONG

BLESSING

Leader: Go forth in the miracle of the grace of God.
And may you be touched
by the fire of the Spirit,
the gentleness of the Christ
and the wisdom of your Maker.

People: **Amen.**

For my forebears of the Clan McRae – the children of grace who, according to the stories, produced many priests, poets and people who defended to the death the things in which they believed.

Index of themes

(This index is not exhaustive. It indicates places where the particular theme is treated at some length. Many of the themes recur throughout the book.)

Aboriginal concerns, 30, 55
Agape meal
 (meal of fellowship), 92
Aloneness, 50
Australia, 65
Beginnings, 11, 15, 18, 20, 23, 26, 30, 33, 51, 55, 59
Birth of a Child, 11
Celebrating Creation, 106
Child with disability, 117
Community, 26, 30, 52, 89
Courage, 26, 96
Cross-cultural unity, 30
Dance of Life, 112
Death, 76, 103, 112, 121
Easter, 76, 80
Endings, 117, 121, 125
Expectation, 39, 87
Faith, 48
Fear, 26, 57, 59
Freedom, 87, 106, 112
Grieving, 42, 103, 117
God serving us, 109
Healing, 44, 103
Honouring God, 100
Hope, 39, 87, 89
Hours of the day, 39, 42, 44, 48, 50, 52, 55, 57, 59
Justice, 30

Marginalised people, 55, 96
Marriage, 18
Mission, 72
Moments in life, 23, 39
Moving, 57, 59
Nearness of God, 65, 69, 87, 109
New journey, 20, 25, 59
Nurture, 44
Passion of God, 125
Praying, 69
Relationships, 18, 26, 33, 52, 89
Renewal, 15, 80
Rest, 48
Risk, 57
Voice of God, 55, 125

Index of resources for worship

Affirmation of faith, 16, 21, 24, 27, 34, 40, 42, 45, 48, 51, 55, 66, 70, 74, 78, 81, 90, 93, 97, 101, 104, 107, 110, 113, 118, 126

Anointing, 105

Assurance of pardon, 16, 20, 24, 27, 34, 39, 44, 50, 53, 57, 60, 66, 73, 81, 87, 93, 97, 100, 107, 110, 113, 126

Blessing and dismissal, 14, 17, 22, 25, 28, 32, 35, 41, 43, 47, 49, 51, 54, 56, 58, 68, 71, 75, 79, 83, 88, 95, 99, 102, 105, 108, 111, 114, 120, 124, 128

Breaking of bread, 46, 82, 97

Call to worship, 44, 59, 76, 106

Commissioning/Sending out, 25, 31, 35, 61, 88, 91, 95, 99, 108

Committal, 123

Declaration, 18

Dedication, 102

Final thanksgiving, 47

Great thanksgiving, 46, 98

Greeting, 23, 26, 30, 33, 44, 59, 72,

Litanies, 49, 53

Memorial Prayer, 99

Offering, 31, 58, 98, 102

Opening sentences, 11, 15, 20, 26, 33, 39, 42, 48, 50, 52, 57, 65, 69, 72, 87, 89, 92, 96, 100, 103, 109, 112, 117, 121, 125

Prayers of confession, 17, 44, 72, 104, 106

Prayers of intercession, 31, 35, 40, 45, 49, 51, 60, 67, 70, 74, 82, 101, 108

Readings, 16, 34, 40, 45, 50, 53, 58, 60, 73, 76, 77, 81, 110, 122

Testimony, 16, 45

Thanksgiving, 13, 99, 101

The Word, 21, 24, 27, 31, 42, 45, 48, 55, 66, 69, 87, 90, 93, 97, 100, 103, 107, 113, 118, 126

The Institution, 99

Witness, 45, 50, 55